HIERARCHY
L*O*VE

THE GUIDE *to help you get the best of someone's love*

KENYA L COLEMAN

NEW YORK

HIERARCHY *of* LOVE
THE GUIDE *to help you get the best of someone's love*

by KENYA L COLEMAN
© 2013 Kenya L. Coleman. All rights reserved.

ISBN 978-1-61448-131-7 Paperback
ISBN 978-1-61448-132-4 eBook
Library of Congress Control Number: 2011937609

Published by:
MORGAN JAMES PUBLISHING
The Entrepreneurial Publisher
5 Penn Plaza, 23rd Floor
New York City, New York 10001
(212) 655-5470 Office
(516) 908-4496 Fax
www.MorganJamesPublishing.com

Cover Design by:
Rachel Lopez
www.r2cdesign.com

Interior Design by:
Bonnie Bushman
bbushman@bresnan.net

In an effort to support local communities, raise awareness and funds, Morgan James Publishing donates a percentage of all book sales for the life of each book to Habitat for Humanity Peninsula and Greater Williamsburg.

Get involved today, visit
www.MorganJamesBuilds.com.

Habitat
for Humanity®
Peninsula and
Greater Williamsburg
Building Partner

TABLE OF CONTENTS

WHY DID I WRITE THIS BOOK?

Simply put, love is difficult but I love, love. More often than not, the laws of attraction are unequally divided. It is an unfortunate but well-known fact that often times; one person is madly in love while the other is not. Yet, they are in a relationship with each other. Not every couple is together because they can't imagine life apart. Not every married person feels like they have found their "soul mate". Even if they once did, there are times when something gets lost along the way. I'm not the first to try to figure it out. Despite all the studies and all the theories, we are still confused. Maybe we don't know all the answers because we haven't heard all the questions. How do we get the most out of our relationship? What does it mean to work on the relationship? If you don't know how to fix your problems where do you begin with this "work"? Well, after much time and consideration, I've proposed a theory in attempt to answer one question. How do we get the best of someone's love?

You might be wondering, what qualifies me to answer this question? Well I'm no authority on the subject of love that's for sure. For one, I sincerely believe that the best inventions come out of the greatest needs. That said, I have had my share of problems like anyone else, probably more. However, I find that my problems differ from most. It's a long story but I'll try to keep it brief. Contrary to the general ideas about women, when it comes to matters of the heart, mine is difficult to touch. I'm not easily impressed. I'm not very emotional. I'm not attracted to looks alone. I'm not even a big fan of cuddling. The guy has to really bring that out of me. If a man does impress me with what he has accomplished, it is not enough to keep my attention. He's got to back it up with some substance. I've been told I'm unaffectionate, disconnected, difficult to figure out...etc. To woo me is to unlock a highly complex code. This has been a huge problem in my relationships including in my marriage...both of them. I have had good relationships in that I have never been in an abusive relationship. I have always been friends with the person I am dating. I can honestly say that in most of my relationships I was treated like a princess, even my first boyfriend when I was just a teenager was very good to me. Some of the friendships I established in those relationships lasted well after the relationships ended.

I know it does not sound like there is a problem, so you may be wondering, what is the problem? The answer to that question is what I had to uncover for myself. However, what I never had a problem doing is attracting the man, keeping the man, and having him fall in love with me. Although my relationships have the appearance of perfection from the outside, on the inside the connection is lacking something for me. It often left me questioning is it them or is it me? One thing is for sure, if I have a common problem in every relationship I'm doing something wrong. I realized that in order for me to fix the problem I have to get to its source. To do that, I had to take inventory of myself to find what makes me continually attract this situation. In the friendship zone, my relationships shine. When it comes to intimacy, affection, passion or even sensitivity, those feelings, for me, are not easily inspired. I thought that perhaps I was dead inside, maybe incapable of loving deeply. I certainly did love my husband of ten years, but something was clearly missing. We just didn't gel in the ways I thought we should have after almost twelve years of life together. With all the talk about love, I was under the impression that everyone was feeling something I just could not feel. I later learned two things; one, not everyone who claims to be in love really is, and two, I am capable of falling in love. I just happen to respond better to someone who I connect with on all levels. In short, I know what I want. While that is a good thing it can also wreak havoc on my relationship if I settle for someone who falls short of that. However, I fooled myself into thinking that if one aspect of the relationship is good it will make up for those things that are not. That has never been true. I've been selling myself short, and unequally paired. For those of you who read the Holy Bible you may be familiar with the term "unequally yoked". For those of you who do not, I'll try to clarify it for you. When two animals are connected by a yoke or a harness they should be connected at a point that allows them ease of motion. That would be equally yoked. If they are connected at awkward points, say, facing opposite directions, then mobility is difficult. They will exhaust themselves trying to move even short distances. Neither of them will make any productive movements unless they work in cooperation. That is unequally yoked. That is what I've felt in most of my relationships. Although I knew what I wanted I didn't expect anyone to be able to deliver. In essence, I lowered my standards of expectation so they fit into the realm of reality…But, the heart wants what it wants, and sooner or later those voids will manifest in some form or another.

After many years of self-inventory combined with life experiences, and analyzing others relationships as well as my own, I have learned that love is complex because it has layers. It is not one dimension. It is as multi-dimensional as the people it connects. As I learned about myself, I began to have a better understanding of love. I have a better understanding of the process, and how it relates to personal growth. The common problem for me in my relationships was my own lack of passion and enthusiasm. For some people, women in particular, it is the lack of affection towards them. For others, the common problem may be abuse, verbal or physical. Whatever the problem, if you are commonly in a relationship that just does not fit, then you clearly don't know your size. In order to get a better understanding of a recurring problem you have to get a better understanding of the source, which is you. My vantage point is from the perspective of someone who is hard to please. My void did not come from not having someone to love me. My void came from the lack of desire to give love. It does the heart good to want to give love. It is the giving of love that is the essence of love.

Imagine that you have a treasure chest that was difficult to unlock. You can't unlock it. You don't know what tools to use. In the process of trying, you tirelessly try tool after tool. You exhaust almost all your resources and invest countless hours trying. Finally, you find a tool that opens the chest. You will not only remember the process of trying, but you will make a note that describes the tool that finally opened it. The specificity of that tool would be a treasure in and of itself. Writing this book has been a treasure for me. In the process of dissecting the barriers that block my own heart, I was able to outline a path for yours to follow. I hope and pray that for you, this will be a road well traveled.

PROLOGUE

$\mathcal{A}$s much as we love, love, it is not enough. That's right! Love alone is not enough to hold a relationship together. In addition to loving one another, a couple needs to like one another, be attracted to one another, respect one another and want to commit to one another. I'm going to go out on a limb and assume that you are reading this book from one of three perspectives. One, you are currently or frequently emotionally detached in your relationship(s). That means you don't attract the kind of mate that really appeals to you, which means you're just going through the motions. Two, you tend to get into relationships with people who don't stay attached to you. That means you can't seem to get your mate to want to commit to you. The third perspective is one where you are in a relationship and it started out good but overtime something got lost. Now the fate of the relationship is leaning toward category one or two. I can most certainly relate to two of the three. After much long-suffering, and many years pondering, I had an epiphany. I already knew that love is not a one size fits all kind of connection. The question is; why is disconnection a recurring problem? In order to figure out what parts of me control my heart and what parts don't, I had to dig deep into myself. I then discovered why part of me feels satisfied and other parts of me don't. I developed this theory of love that helped me learn my size. Not only do we not want a one size fits all relationship but what we want is a custom fit. My theory of love outlines love as a whole and helps point out the characteristics that make it personal.

Hierarchy, if you don't know, is defined as, "a group of persons or things arranged in order of rank." In my opinion, true love has many levels. It is my belief that, we possess many different emotions, and each emotion responds to its own individual set of character traits. Just as personalities are multi-facetted, the aspects that appeal to us are also multi-facetted. In addition to that, there are basic traits that serve as the glue that bond people in relationships. Those traits are Sex Appeal, Friendship, Trust, and Respect. These are the four parts of appeal. These traits are basic to the needs of all relationships and the characteristics that fulfill them are different for each individual. What makes a person sexy, who we call friend, and what characteristics in a person cause us to have respect for them, all have different qualifications, specific to individual personalities. When we meet the conditions, we get the desired response from that person of interest. For example, if you are a woman who is an excellent cook, those characteristics alone will not make you sexually appealing. Those qualities may make a man want you in his life, especially if he's a big eater. However, if you want more from him than his "compliments to the chef", you're going to need more than dinner to bring it out of him. On the other-hand, maybe you are very good looking, you have a nice body and you are a sharp dresser, that is not enough to make a person want to marry you. You may be a giving person with all the best intentions but that may not earn you the respect you are hoping to get…You get the point!

Emotional needs are hierarchical because large needs, which serve as foundational needs, must be fulfilled before we are emotionally mature enough to fulfill, for ourselves, or for others any higher-level need. In support of that, there are hosts of components that accompany those needs to make them complete. To put it in other words, there are requirements to meet before the need is satisfied. The byproduct can be a fulfilling partnership and even a lasting, loving, relationship. Like building a house, you can't build your roof before you build the foundation. Things have an order of operation because the order is necessary to ensure the strength and stability of the house. This book is written to show, first the needs that serve as the core, then the requirements that fulfill each need. You can think of my philosophy of love's hierarchy as a metaphorical house. I will explain how one level can support and determine the strength, presence or lack of, its successive level. Each component within that level is an extension to complete its general characteristics. In a hierarchy, lower level needs are at the foundation and should be satisfied before higher-level ones can be satisfied. Everyone's preference is different according to their personality, life experiences and so on. Therefore, the other levels may be interchangeable in its position of importance for each individual. Level one, however, is by far the biggest and most important of all…for all, that is self-love.

Many people fall in and out of love many times over and quite often become discouraged and leave one bad relationship after another never having experienced true love. Subsequently, they end up building up defenses against falling in love and end up entering into the following relationship with defensive behaviors. Those defensive behaviors set up barriers that make it impossible to form a partnership, which is a disservice to both parties. Anyone who is interested in being in a relationship should know what real love encompasses, and be able to decipher, real, from...well, that other feeling. Having said that, let me also say this, I am not claiming to give some sort of formula for changing a loveless relationship into one of deep passionate love. I may be able to help you figure out what is wrong with the relationship you are currently in and enlighten you so you can make an informed decision about your love life and the future of your relationships moving forward.

My desire is to inspire a deeper look into what most perceive to be love. We will explore what love really is by definition, and discuss what characteristics apply. I hope that once you have read this book in its entirety, you will be better able to determine what is missing in your current relationship. Hopefully, you will be able to determine the exact source of the problem. It is my intent to help you learn some things about yourself that may influence the possibility of experiencing fulfilling love. Perhaps together we can determine if you have it or if you ever experienced it at all. My desire is that by the completion of this book, you will have gained first; "food for thought", second; revelation of both, past and present relationships, and third; some clarity on that thing you thought was love that turned out so wrong. You may also possibly gain a new perception of your personal needs, and a stronger sense of self-awareness. In fact, if I were to attempt to give a formula for making love work I would say that most importantly it works better when both parties have a strong sense of self-awareness. The relationship is stronger when both parties are comfortable in their own skin, confident in themselves, and have a plan for themselves and their future, as individuals before they meet. That is indeed the pre-requisite for a happier union, two emotionally mature, spiritually grounded individuals. Then finally, you may be able to determine what traits of the opposite sex truly compliment you. Then you may be able to recognize, be ready for, and receive, real and lasting love.

WHAT IS LOVE,
REALLY?

WHAT IS LOVE, REALLY?

Before I go any further, I must give a clear and concise break down of the subject at hand. I must do this because we use this word so casually it has lost something overtime. "I love this record". "I love that dress". Certainly, if we can throw it around so easily to describe inanimate objects, it comes even easier when we are describing another person with feelings and emotions like us. However, do we really love everyone we claim to love? Better yet, has everyone who has claimed to love us really loved us?

The dictionary's definition of love, in short, is, *"A profoundly tender, passionate, deep affection for another person"*. That does get to the point but it is vague when compared to the biblical definition of love, 1corinthians13:4-6, paraphrased: *Love is patient, love is kind, it does not envy nor brag in attempt to show off. It isn't proud, rude or self-serving. It isn't easily angered and it keeps no record of wrongs. Love does not take into account the evil (which it suffers). It does not rejoice at the iniquity (injustice) but rejoices with the truth, endures all things, hopes all things. Love perseveres.* That is a heap of explanation for such a little word. Perhaps it is not so little a word after all, and for the purposes of this book it is the more appropriate definition. Love has too much depth to simplify its definition.

Many of us have felt tender, passionate deep affection for one person or another, but then it changed or we ended up hurt, bitter, and disappointed. A couple of things could have been the case; one is, maybe, you were in love with some one who didn't love you. Then you have to ask yourself what did you really love about them if they didn't love you? Another thing that could've been the case is, maybe someone you thought highly of showed you interest and it gave you a self esteem boost. In affect, you became more and more hungry for their attention and that kind hunger stirs up feelings that may be mistaken for love. I use these two scenarios because they are the ones with which I am most familiar. Can you relate better to the first scenario? When you broke up did you understand? Did you wish them well or were you bitter and hoped they would be miserable without you? It is human nature to be upset and even wish them bad initially. We may all be guilty of that now and again but...Well you see, the definition of love says love is not self-serving. Love does not hold a record of wrong. That means you will eventually understand that it is not about you. Then you will be able to rejoice in that person's true happiness even if they are not with you. If the second scenario is one you relate to then, like the first, it is a very self-serving and yet self-destructive response. Neediness and wanting to be wanted is not love but may be a lack of self-confidence or the result of past experiences. Hardships in life can create feelings of emptiness that drive you to fill that emotional void. Neediness will however drive you to be more affectionate and more attentive and available to someone in an effort to solicit the return of affection or attentiveness. Although it may stir up your emotions and make you feel warm and fuzzy it is not a healthy situation. Frankly, convincing yourself that any affection shown to you is a sign of love makes you vulnerable. It heightens the possibility of you subsequently thinking you are in love again and again. You don't have to play hard to get, you just need not to be too easy to get. The one thing I've learned about love…true love…is that it is more about, how good you want to make someone feel rather than how good you need them to make you feel. It is more about the desire to show affection than it is about the need to receive it.

If you imagine a mother and child, the love a mother has for her child is so profound she'll sacrifice her own comfort for the sake of her child's. She doesn't do it because she wants the child to praise her for it. Usually the child never knows all she gives of herself for his sake. All she wants for her baby is the best life has to offer. She sacrifices to make that happen for him without soliciting his praise or thanks. His joy is her fulfillment even if others find it difficult to see good in him and he is in the eyes of most, a terrible person, she wants good for him. It is never about how he makes her feel—That is love! Similarly just as between mother and child that kind of unconditional love is possible between man and woman, that selfless lasting love.

With all its complexity why do we even bother, why do we even have such a strong desire to find love? It is a scientific fact that feelings of love heighten responses in the brains neurotransmitter similar to euphoric inducing drugs such as cocaine. In essence, love is literally like a drug. Love heightens feelings of euphoria and stirs up many emotions in us, feel-good emotions that is. Even with the possibility of heartache and pain, we all have an innate need for love. If you have ever experienced it, you cannot help wanting nothing less. If you cannot relate to this feeling of elation, then you clearly have not been in love. One sign to know you are in love is that you lose interest in other objects of attraction. We are all subject to fall. The only defense against falling in love is to be in love already. I believe that many of us have not discovered it because we get in our own way, but it is not a thing to enter into lightly. Its euphoric effects can cause you to make poor choices if you are not emotionally mature. I want you to know the characteristics of love. It will continue to be hard to find if you don't have an adequate description. Once you have a description, you will know when to reel it in and when you need to throw it back. It is not enough to spend your time with a good person but you want the right person, the one that fits you.

The first key to giving and receiving love is to first love your self. You cannot truly love anyone and trust that you can receive love in return if you do not love yourself. That is why much of this book is about you. Before we can explore love for anyone, we must first examine where we are with ourselves. All that said, now we can begin

Level One
(THE FOUNDATION)

SELF LOVE

SELF LOVE

*I*f we are building a house of love, "self love" is our strong foundation it keeps our house stable. It strengthens the structure at the source so that nothing we pile on top will break the house. The stronger the foundation, the less likely it is to be carried away by storm. Does that make sense to you? This is the first and most important level because if you are not valuable to yourself you will not allow anyone to love you, nor can you truly love anyone. You will not feel like you truly deserve their love. You may even feel suspicious about every good deed they do for you as though they are up to something, "why are they being so nice?" Before long, this kind of attitude will sabotage any future acts of kindness toward you. Many relationship problems are the product of low self-esteem. Jealousy, possessiveness, promiscuity and even abuse are all the result of insecurities. In addition to that, low self-esteem is a very unattractive personality trait. When you are secure within yourself, you are not as likely to become the perpetrator of the previously mentioned circumstances. However, you may still experience this in your relationship if your mate is not as secure as you. In essence, a healthy self-image, and a high morale is the foundation for a strong and healthy relationship.

After all, in order to have a partnership with someone you must be a good partner yourself.

There is a fine line between high self-esteem and conceit. It is my opinion that conceited people are merely acting out to conceal their insecurities. Conceit is an excessive, exaggerated opinion of ones self, and this personality usually needs the support of an audience's "oohs and awes" to believe in himself. Vanity and conceit are equally unattractive qualities that can later render an unfavorable response. However, confidence in one's self is freeing and it fosters an optimistic perspective on life. It is not pretentious, and it is also very attractive. A confident person may find himself being admired and respected by many people, without even trying. A truly confident person is intrinsically motivated with or without the company or even support of others. A confident person does not automatically see himself as the victim in an unfortunate situation but to the contrary, may already have a back-up plan in line. A confident person has no problem making others feel good. They exude a positive energy that attracts and inspires others.

When it comes down to it, how do you rate yourself? Are you only as good as the relationship you are in, or are you valuable with or without a relationship? Do you rate yourself according to how popular you are? Do you find people gravitate toward you or try to avoid you? Here is the hard one. Do you usually find yourself in love all too frequently, and even more frequently in a relationship with someone who does not share your feelings? Imagine the beauty of a relationship between two people who already felt complete before they ever met. It is important that you feel like a whole person before you seek a mate. I cannot stress that enough! Entering into a relationship too needy can push a person away. In fact, they might run away and avoid any contact with you. It is psychologically taxing and emotionally draining for the other person. In addition to that, it's unfair. Simply put, it is a recipe for a disaster.

Confidence is not just about believing in yourself or feeling like you are "all that", that is the misconception many people have (particularly people who are faking confidence). It is really about having peace in one's spirit. It is when you have reached a place where you know what your good qualities are and you embrace your bad qualities as well. It is when; you are able to embrace all things that make you, you. You know you are made of many qualities and just one of them is not enough to define you. You appreciate your path in life, your energy and motivation comes from within even when you are alone. The sense of peace makes you comfortable in your own skin. Other people's accomplishments serve as an educational tool that simply sparks ideas, not jealousy. It is when you truly believe that "He that is in you is greater than he that is in the world". Negative commentary from others motivate you instead of bring you down. Confidence enables you to accept rejection as a cue to go in another direction and keep moving forward instead of defeat you. A confident person does not need someone to hold his/her hand to make it through every task, because your inner strength gives you the assurance that you can handle it. Confident people do not need someone to validate their ideas because they understand that people may not understand their vision. They understand that innovators and new ideas are often misunderstood. Confidence allows you to present yourself to others, composed and comfortable. It demands respect, it attracts attention, and it is very sexy. You might be the one quiet person in a crowded room and yet you stand out and people feel compelled to approach you. The truth is, not everyone has "it" and when people see someone who does, they want to know you better. People with low self-esteem are deceived by their own inflated perception of everyone else. They see themselves less valuable or not as good by comparison. No matter how perfect someone looks, everyone has struggles. Everyone feels unsure at times. Low self-esteem says, I don't look like everyone else therefore, they won't like me. High self-esteem says, I don't look like everyone else because I'm me and I'm not supposed to. A person with low self-esteem takes their differences and sees them as character flaws. The person with high self-esteem takes those differences and embraces being unique.

The difference between low self-esteem and high self-esteem is the depth of personal perception. How many good qualities do you think you have? How valuable are those qualities in your world, according to you? If you are a person with beautiful hair and eyes and everyone compliments your hair and eyes, is that the sum of who you are? Suppose you lose your hair or your eyes become disfigured? Was that all you had going for you? You have to imagine that you are made of lots of valuable layers. Even in the unfortunate event some layers may be lost, you still have plenty of valuable ones left. You were not created to just blend in. Your life has purpose. Your unique qualities are a valued asset to the human race. You are wasting valuable time waddling in self-pity. Your negative opinion of yourself will influence everyone else's opinion of you. What you may not realize is, people don't think badly of you until you convince them they should. In many cases people who talk bad about you don't do so because they actually think bad of you. Most likely, they really admire you. The problem may be that the thought of you makes them look at themselves with disappointment, therefore, you are not likable to them. Try to keep that in mind and don't take all the negative commentary so personal. It may truly be a reflection of admiration. Unfortunately that is how admiration from a person with no self-respect is delivered.

Throughout this chapter, we will take inventory of self. Perhaps you will discover that you are getting in your own way of finding real love. This can be the case for even the person with a healthy self-image, sometimes we just become too hard on ourselves and we settle for less than we know we are worth. Perhaps we just stop believing, the right one exists. In any case, there are obstacles to overcome.

What Are Your Best Assets?

If you are going to measure your self-worth, then it is most important to assess what composes that image. This is important for more reasons than one. One reason is, the way that you see yourself influences the image you project for others to see. Another reason is, if you have built your self-image solely based on what others think of you then you are subject to a state of confusion. People and their opinions will pull and push you everywhere but to your destiny. It is also important not to base your total self-image according to your physical attributes. You should know this factor is highly volatile and subject to change. A healthy self-image should be the harvest of things such as, your faith, your God given gifts, your wisdom, your discipline, your ambition, etc.

Knowing your God given gifts is pertinent to finding your own destiny. Finding your own destiny is essential to finding a life of fulfillment. Fulfilled individuals, on the path towards their own destiny are likely to have a greater discernment about what to look for, or be receptive to, in a relationship. You are more ambitious about life when you do what fulfills you. You get adrenalin from within, the outcome is better and it is less laborious. Let's examine the word fulfill a little closer, it means to develop the full potential of. If utilizing your God given gifts leads you toward your destiny and your destiny gives your life fulfillment, then it is in your best interest to find and use your gifts. This is your number one asset. Note, God given gifts will not fall into a category of unlawful or immoral deeds even if you find yourself good at such things, there are much greater things in you. You might say, "Well my gift isn't making me any money and I've got to work". "There is no time for me to be playing around with any hobbies". In that case, I'll advise you to try to find time to do what you love, on your time off. It will turn out to be more therapeutic than not.

For example, if you love to dance, you're not likely to find many jobs, if any, in the classifieds as a dancer but find a class that allows you to express your love for dance. Don't equate your passion for things with monetary gain. Make time to do what you love even if only to express yourself. This is how you will discover those valuable layers of yourself. Paint those portraits even if you never sell any. Write that book even if no one ever reads it. Decorate your friends' houses free if you desire to be an interior designer and cannot get work. Do these things in your spare time. You may even find that your drive and perseverance will open doors for you in your desired field. If you're wondering, what does this have to do with recognizing or finding true love? The answer is, "Plenty!" You cannot allow responsibilities to govern every aspect of your life any more than you can go through life living irresponsibly. There must be balance. Balance brings peace of mind and peace of mind is priceless! When you are at peace with yourself, you are not as likely to be desperately seeking love. A desperate person seeking love is more likely unable to see the relationship for what it is. If it is a bad match, you may not able to see it or be as willing to accept it and let go. It is best that you are content with your life alone before committing to, or even seeking to be in a relationship.

I am not saying you should not desire intimacy. Our creator gave us these feelings as a gift, nonetheless, just as with any urges we are expected and required to exercise some discipline. At the very least, you should know who you are. Moreover, you should know your potential before making any major commitments such as parenthood or marriage. Marriage and parenthood can be two of the most life altering, joys life can offer. They can also become two of the biggest burdens of your life, if entered into lightly and unprepared. Both require constant time, effort, and most of all, sacrifice. This is not something that is always clear to see when you look at other people. From the outside of a situation all we see is beautiful babies and husbands kissing their wives as they go off to work for the day, Mr. and Mrs. On the checks and we look at it and say "awe, I want that." What we don't see are the struggles they go through everyday just to make two different opinions and personality traits merge as one. The merger requires some bit of effort, from both parties, maybe all day every day for years and years. This is important to consider when you feel desperate to be in a loving relationship. Remember it is love you want, not the look of love. Don't sell yourself short if it is love you really want. Hold out for the real thing it is out there for you. Develop your skills, your talents, and get your degree. Build yourself to a place where you feel confident about both the inner and outer you. Make your self a much more valuable player in the relationship game.

Again, I do not profess to be giving the keys to having a perfect relationship. That's not realistic— there isn't one. However, what there is, is someone perfect for you and the best way to make room for that special someone is to clear out the confusion about self. In the state that the world is in today, we cannot afford to keep trying lovers on for size, swapping them out like library books. In addition to that, how many times can we keep promising God I'll love this person till death do us part? You only have one life yet you've had five marriages.

It is time to take inventory of self. Stop, think, what are you looking for in a mate? For the most part, it is human nature to seek balance, even if we don't recognize it as balance that we're seeking. For example, it's been said that pretty, "girly" girls like bad boys. Why is that? Well it's not the fact that "pretty girls" are not attracted unless the man is a convicted felon. What it is in fact, is just as long legs, high heels, and curves, are synonymous with all things female; roughness, fearlessness and strength are the depiction of "all man." This is more likely to be true for teenagers to young adults. Middle aged women and older have a different definition of what is "all man." The point is, in our quest for balance, we tend to seek what we do not possess or crave that which we are deficient. If a relationship is going to have a fair chance at longevity, we can't enter into it feeling inadequate and emotionally void. The voids are fewer when you are at peace with yourself. That said, the more we lack in ourselves the more we extract from our mate.

Now let's paint a clearer picture. A young woman—we'll call her Marjorie—twenty years of age, has been working at the neighborhood library for three years now. Marjorie got this job through her high school work-study program, in her senior year at age seventeen. She also had a baby that year. Unfortunately, the baby's father is not in the picture she hasn't seen him since high school. Marjorie didn't have the luxury of family support. She was raised by a single parent and has four younger siblings. All her mother can offer her is a place to live. Marjorie has thought about college but doesn't have a clue about what she wants to be in life. She hasn't really had time to entertain that thought, because she dove straight into major responsibilities during her adolescent years. She's at a point now where she has to give so much of herself before she has even developed a dream much less a plan. Life becomes a series of routine responsibilities and it seems she can't find much peace at home. Mom is still the boss there! She's even dictating how Marjorie should care for her own baby. Marjorie sees fit to get her own place. "I can manage if I budget my money right, I just got a raise." Once she moves into her own place, she sees so many factors she hadn't considered. "This living on my own thing is harder than I thought." She starts to figure that the missing piece to her puzzling life is companionship. A man with a good job, somebody to help me pay these bills and take some of this load off me, she thinks.

The first problem with Marjorie is her lack of personal development. The pressures of life's immediate responsibilities have overshadowed it. Now the focus is to relieve the pressure. Not only does she not see the importance of self-development right now, but she is also ignorant about the amount of energy a relationship will pull from her at this vulnerable stage in her life. She figures, if a lack of finances is the problem, a man with a job is a solution. Seeking a mate as an answer at a desperate time is clearly the wrong answer.

For the sake of simplifying things as much as possible, let's just say she meets a man, we'll call him Ian. He's a moderately attractive man, twenty-five years old. He's nice to Marjorie and her baby; in fact, he and the baby have a tighter bond than he and Marjorie. She is happy about that at first. In addition to that, he's willing to help with the bills. Before she knows it he's there all the time and eventually it's home— This is beautiful!—A storybook romance! They look so adorable together— Everyone says so! He's picking the baby up from daycare on his way home from work and it appears to be the sweetest thing. As time goes by Marjorie and Ian realize all they really have in common is this apartment and these bills. They can't seem to get along. Every conversation turns into an argument so they just stop talking. He begins to stay out later and later and some days not come home at all. Marjorie is frustrated and sad a lot. She suspects he's cheating on her and she discovers she's pregnant again. At this point finances are not the only deficiency, she needs a man to make her forget about the current man in her life. Thus begins the cycle of one bad relationship after another. Marjorie's problem before she met Ian was not that she needed a man to take care of her. In her under developed emotional and psychological state, she allowed desperate times to determine her decisions. Not only was she not ready for all the responsibilities she piled on herself, but she was trying to find balance with a young man equally as under developed as she. A recipe for disaster!

Allow yourself to move past your emotions attached to the former relationship. The excitement you initially felt in this relationship may have been sparked simply because he is opposite of that other person. That can feel very refreshing soon after a break-up. When you are in that rebound state of mind you cannot see the whole picture. Once you have fully recovered from the former relationship, you can make connections with a clean emotional pallet. That is why I propose the importance of personal development. It is essential for you to be at a place in your life where you are emotionally mature. Emotional maturity helps you to be able to make decisions responsibly instead of emotionally. It is also very important that your life or the life you build with someone does not impede your personal growth. If you are in a well-rounded relationship and you are developing in it, then work through the complications. God willing, you will be together "until death due you part". If that relationship should fail, don't jump into another relationship right away. You run the risk of perpetuating a cycle of bad relationships, one after the other. The problem then becomes that you are making poor choices based on your temporary emotional state. Some of those choices could produce life long consequences. Allow yourself time to heal from the past relationship. Allow yourself some time to further develop and grow emotionally, spiritually, financially, etc. When the thought of the past relationships no longer evokes any emotions, then you are ready to move on. That is, when you think about your relationships, especially the most recent break-up, you are not angry, sad, frustrated or even turned on anymore. Let's say, hypothetically, you were in a relationship for years with someone who abused you mentally and physically. When you broke up you were timid with low self-esteem, and financially struggling. You then meet a man who is gentle, financially stable and speaks to you with respect and you feel like you are falling in love. Your emotions stir up a false-positive simply because he is so opposite of the person before. This does not make him the man for you. The two of you may have nothing at all in common. Surely, after spending time with someone completely opposite of "the monster" you will heal but when that smoke clears you will find yourself smack in the middle of another mess and you never saw it coming. Allowing yourself time to develop will help you make better choices for your life, free from the confusion of temporary emotions. If you are in a relationship or continue to be in a relationship that is lacking more than it produces, you need to know where to start if you are going to save it. On the other hand, if it is not worth it, you need to know when to move on. Life is too short and time is too precious to remain in a dead end relationship. Don't waste time trying to convince your self that a lackluster relationship will blossom into something wondrous. It will not. If you are not feeling the love there probably isn't any and it's not the end of the world. Don't be afraid to move on, new beginnings can be wonderful.

The Importance Of Intrinsic Motivation

Intrinsic; "*to belong to a thing by its very nature*". Motive; "*the goal or object of one's actions*". Simply put, it is the importance of encouraging yourself to set and accomplish goals independent of outside influences. This is profoundly powerful if we could just grasp it. How many times have you heard someone say, "I wish I would've done ... If I would've just had the support of my family"? Perhaps you have even experienced a feeling of excitement about a vision or dream and told a friend or family member that did not share your ambitions and you got discouraged. It happens to the best of us, but how many dreams are you going to let die because other people's lack of vision? Maybe they are not as creative and assertive as you are. Do not allow someone else's pessimistic perspective on life suffocate and kill your ambitious spirit. Embody a spirit of perseverance that grows in negativity. Use it as fuel to drive you further. Remember, the haters really do love you, they just don't understand you. The more they say "you can't have it" let it drive you to excellence. This is exactly the kind of motivation that will bring God's plan for your life to fruition. I do advise against surrounding yourself with too many pessimistic people. There is a limit to how much negativity you can actually use as fuel. Too much negativity can weigh you down.

There is an old cliché "misery loves company." People do love company, so do not keep company with negative pessimistic people and there are quite a few in every crowd. Find some people who inspire you to grow and be a better you. Separate yourself from people who stay in a rut. You are no super hero, and you do not have enough energy and ambition to accomplish a dream for you and a dream for them. Pray for them, give a helping hand if you can and keep moving. I am not suggesting that you abandon a friend or relative in need. Nor am I suggesting that if someone requires full time care, that you should turn your back on them. I am referring to those able body individuals who can do but lack either the vision or the desire to reach for something greater. If it is your gift to help people realize their potential then you will be blessed operating in that role. However, if your gifts point you in a completely different direction then you must stay true to yourself. A life filled with feelings of regret is a bitter one.

If you are a person who needs the approval of others before you can make a final decision on something, or if you are someone who needs praise from others for everything you accomplish in life, it is you I am speaking to the loudest. If you are proud of yourself, why isn't your own praise good enough for you? Do you think so little of yourself that everyone else's opinion of your work matters more than your own? You may say, "How can I achieve intrinsic motivation?" You can simply make a decision to do your best at everything and be proud of yourself for that. Even if you do not achieve success right away keep working on your craft. Thomas Edison, while trying to perfect his invention of the light bulb made thousands of mistakes. In the words of Edison, as it is written in his autobiography *"I have gotten lots of results! If I find 10,000 ways something won't work, I haven't failed. I am not discouraged, because every wrong attempt discarded is often a step forward....."* I could not have said that better my self. That is a profound statement. Keep that in mind to encourage yourself. The more you learn what not to do the closer you get to getting it just right. Do not look for someone's praises to help you get through. If you pay close enough attention, you may find that those very people from whom you seek your approval do not have all the answers. They too have their own struggles and shortcomings. It is always okay to seek someone's advice but ask yourself, why are you seeking their advice? Are they wiser than you are? Are they an authority on the subject? Do you just want to impress them or want them to like you? Be very careful if it is the third, not to let their response affect or influence your goals. Your drive to achieve must come from within. You cannot go after the dream mama has for you, or what everybody else told you, you should pursue. You will create a long confusing path only to get so far down the road to realize you left yourself miles ago. Do not lose you, in your efforts to try to impress someone else.

Intrinsic motivation is an essential element in the personal developmental process. While our God does put people in our paths to impart some things to us, it is still our responsibility to be able to recognize who those people are. Not everyone has a good word for you! Do not assume that anybody is better at shaping your destiny than you are. No one can know you better than you can, even if you are confused about whom you are. If you believe it to be divine intervention when you meet someone that seems to have all the answers for you, isn't it also highly likely that divine impartation from God, directly to you, also exist? If this sounds foreign to you then you have some growing to do. If you need a leader, it is better to have the spirit of God, lead you. Put in common terms, your intuition and conscious are both things you cannot see or touch but they act as an internal voice that intends to direct you. The more you ignore them the less they speak to you. It is immensely important for you to develop an intimate and personal relationship with God so you also develop wisdom and understanding to differentiate between divine impartation and worldly influence. If you are easily influenced by too many different sources before you can make a decision, you cannot truly be assertive. You're shooting aimlessly at no target. You have to clear your head of bias opinions, negative remarks and selfish or foolish advice. Know that, you have to set realistic goals for yourself. If you are to accomplish any of these goals, you are going to have to assert yourself. Know also that, you will not have a pep squad to follow you every step of the way, if ever. You need to be able to conceptualize, and execute your own plans for your life. Key words *Your Life*. If you accept this responsibility, you have taken control of your own destiny. If you leave it up to someone else to make all the plans, lead the way, and simply take the driver's seat while you go along for the ride you have decided to let things happen rather than make things happen. In this case, you should be humble no matter what the outcome because you have relinquished your own power.

Live with more certainty, encourage yourself all the way to the finish. This is a definite boost for the morale. Getting in tune with you is going to require a lot of quiet time, and lot of alone time. The best way to motivate someone is to support him or her mentally and physically and most importantly, not get in his or her way. The best way to get to know someone is to spend a lot of personal time with them and learn their likes and dislikes. If you are able to do that for any one, do it for you. It is essential for your development.

The Value Of Time Alone

If you are not the kind of person who likes to be alone and you usually find yourself lonely or bored when you are alone then you probably cannot grasp that there can be value in time alone. If that describes you then you should work on a project of some sort when you are alone. Be sure to spend this time wisely. You cannot afford to be idle or unproductive when you are alone, if that setting makes you feel desperate in any way. The idea is that you are able to become familiar with your inner voice, away from outside influences or distractions and comfortable with yourself. This will help you learn your strengths and it will subsequently empower you.

You should in fact plan your activities or a schedule of some kind, in preparation for "you time." This can be somewhat like a date, the only difference is, all the activities have but one participant—you! To really make the most of these experiences it is better not to spend all your alone time watching movies or television. That will serve as outside influence and defeat the purpose unless of course you are watching something that inspires and uplifts you. I will still say not all the time. Try to reach inside yourself and be creative or productive in some way. I must say, I am not suggesting that you should not ever watch simple entertainment television or movies while you are alone, that would be absurd to suggest that. I would like to remind you that the purpose is to find balance. If you have characteristics that are extreme in one direction then you should stretch yourself a bit in the opposite direction to perhaps, snap back somewhere in the middle. This advice may not necessarily fit all situations but as it pertains to being alone with you, it is sound advice. In any healthy relationship, even if two people love spending time together it is likely that the relationship is so successful because each individual is competent and content when they are alone as well. Besides, in life, there is a great chance you may have to experience life alone for one reason or another and this could occur unexpectedly or maybe even gradually, but it is inevitable and usually beyond our control. You will be better able to handle this if people are more companions to you than they are the completion of you.

Examine your reasons for hating to be alone. If you are bored and cannot think of anything to do, this is the time to work on a hobby or pamper your self all day. You could go see a movie and take yourself out to lunch. As long as you made the decisions and you have encouraged and enjoyed your self. The more you enjoy your time alone the less you are likely to be clingy in a relationship. As I mentioned earlier being too clingy or needy is an unattractive trait that creates a negative energy in the relationship. Quite honestly, it is just annoying. One person will feel annoyed which will make the other person feel neglected and resentful.

The goal is to get to a place where you believe in your own abilities to accomplish tasks, transact business and entertain your own mind. You need to see yourself as complete, even while single. This is valuable because the saying that relationships are 50/50 is a myth. Relationships need to be 100/100 each individual needs to bring a full deck to the table. The decks may not be identical but they should both be complete. This is the best way to compliment each other and begin a relationship equally yoked. It would be easier if no one goes into the relationship feeling overwhelmed or as if the relationship is, simply all "take" and no "give". For example, say a woman meets a man, they develop a good friendship, good conversations but physically he is not the type of person she would usually find attractive. He has several businesses that are flourishing and making lots of money, very confident and charming, dresses nice, smells good and is in good physical shape. She is still a student working full time but just making ends meet, in fact she has never even lived on her own. She knows she is an attractive woman but she has never met a man with the finances and the resources this man has. This person can buy her anything and he knows how to conduct himself around people of any social and economic status. She is so impressed with all that she sees in him. She cannot see what he is not. She thinks she is falling in love. He on the other hand thinks she is intelligent and gorgeous. He is not worried about her financial situation because he has the means to provide. He loves her and wants to marry her. She loses focus of her own personal goals. Why not? After all, she is marrying into money. All she needs is to stay pretty and smart and the two of them can live in harmony. Then they get married, her husband suffers from an illness that keeps him from being able to work. He needs multiple surgeries and won't recover for years. The money is depleting because your life style was one of greater means than the current household income. She now has to step up and run things, take care of her husband and the home. He is no longer charming. He is no longer stepping out of a shiny luxury vehicle. Expensive dinners are no longer in the budget. Right now, he is weak out of shape and not that attractive. Her love is fading. She feels overwhelmed with all this responsibility. It is all very unfamiliar. Without him in control of things, she feels like a fish out of water. She just does not want it anymore. He still loves his wife. He treated her well and accepted her with nothing, and has no reason to believe she will bail on him in a time of need. She, on the other hand is completely unhappy. This is not what she signed up for.

This little story may be a little over exaggerated because it all happened in a couple of paragraphs but it is not completely foreign. The first problem is, had she been of equal social and financial status at the beginning of the relationship she might not have been as impressed with things because she's made her own accomplishments. The car, the expensive dates, the social status, it is all very synthetic. Being impressed by someone's accomplishments is helpful when it comes to gaining respect for them but you must be careful not to mistake it for the full package. Things may come and go. You have to ask yourself, are you impressed with the personality that is able to acquire such things, or are you excited about the presence of things? If you love the person because of his work ethic and drive then you love him on the inside. Even if the situation changes a person is likely to still have the same personality traits. The point is, if you accomplish some great things on your own you are more likely to look beyond material gain or social economic status. Those things may cloud your judgment of whether or not that person's character compliments yours.

How Did You Develop Your Self-Image?

Your self-image is important because it determines what kind of people and situations you attract and entertain. What do I mean by this? Well, simply put, I believe we attract the kind of people we feel we deserve. In an effort to discover what, in your opinion, you deserve, we must explore how you developed your image of yourself.

I have spent my entire adult life helping women polish their look and add to their self-image. I have been a professional stylist for twenty-plus years. I've built a rapport with many women over the years. My job as a stylist in many ways put me in the role of a counselor. For many women, a prim polished outer appearance is an essential part of boosting their self-esteem. Many have even said when their hair isn't done they don't feel like themselves. I guess there is something to be said about the power of appearance in the human psyche.

That is something we can attribute to our culture. The images portrayed for what is attractive has us either consciously or unconsciously checking ourselves to see how we measure up. For many of us it is easier to fix the outer self and portray that ideal image, than to fix the inner self. The inner self, now that's the person to whom I am speaking, While it is a good thing to care about your appearance, your good looks or lack thereof, are not the sum of your value. Having been made in the divine image of the creator does not mean that he too, has long hair, brown eyes and a small waist. It does mean that just as he is capable of greatness beyond measure so are you.

I have seen many young girls who have curves beyond their years, who assume that is their best asset. This happens when so many people comment on their physical attributes often. When an impressionable child finds the only positive feedback comes from how she looks in revealing clothes she may become conditioned to believe her body is her greatest asset. She may then begin to solicit that kind of attention by displaying her "assets" more often. She is now wearing tighter clothes and shorter shorts and skirts. For many young girls, this is misconstrued as self-esteem. There is a big difference between genuine confidence and a boosted ego. Soliciting compliments is not a sign of confidence. It is an attempt to boost the ego when confidence is low. Truly, any self-image built based on external factors is as unpromising as those factors. In other words if you have built your self-image solely on the shape of your body, or how nice you look in your clothes that is an unstable image because beauty is fleeting. People may have something good to say about you today and yet tomorrow it may be just the opposite. You can't allow people's opinions define you. I must say, I am one for trying to keep in shape. I am all for keeping oneself well groomed and polished. I intend to fight the aging process every step of the way. I spend a lot of time whitening my teeth, doing my hair, and working out for both health and vanity reasons. I made my living selling the polished physical image. I could not have sold it so well if I did not buy it myself. However, although it is a flattering thing to hear someone say, "You are beautiful" you should never consider that as your best asset. You should really see yourself as more than that!

If your self-value is as shallow as your physical attributes, you are likely to attract someone as shallow as those values. You run the risk of having a relationship that is all about the physical attributes. Beware of fragile yet inflated egos that disguise themselves as confidence. They are not the same! You will be better served to leave your ego out of your relationship. A fragile ego requires continual input from outside sources but self esteem comes from within. No one wants the job of keeping your ego boosted. That job is yours alone. Sexiness is an important component in a relationship for most of us, however; it is merely like an ornament on a tree. Certainly, we like to adorn our tree with beautiful decorations but we first must pick the appropriate tree. In many instances, the nicer the decorations the better the foundational "tree" must be. If we're going to spend so much time shopping for the right ornaments we definitely want a good tree. Right? So the more attractive you are as a person you should have that much more to offer spiritually, mentally and intellectually. Perhaps your attractive features were given to you for the purposes of putting you in contact with lots of people. Since we know that people like, and are drawn to physically beautiful people initially, it is not a gift we are supposed to use frivolously. The operative word being, initially, what impression do you intend to make on them once you encounter them. What will they remember about you when they leave your presence? Most importantly will it be a positive impression.

I spend a lot of time talking about self-image and self-esteem because I believe that it affects most everything we say and do. I believe our own self-image affects the way we represent ourselves and subsequently affects the way others perceive us and ultimately treat us. If you see yourself as a leader, you will operate in leadership and others will naturally follow. If you see yourself as a weak individual, you will find that others take advantage of you and trample over you often. Additionally, if you have no self-respect, then others will not respect you either. This is also true in relationships. If you feel like all men cheat, then you will open the doors and your heart to a cheater. If you feel you are deserving of a man who treats you like his queen, then you will settle for nothing less. You will find the men in your life will treat you with respect and even cater to you. This is even true if the man you meet has cheated on others or mistreated others. It does not mean he will do it to you. Genuine self-respect demands respect in return, even without talking much about it. He will treat you with love and respect or move on to someone he can victimize. Be at peace if he does move on and count it as a blessing. Do not spend a lot of time trying to force what doesn't fit.

Level Two
(THE ELECTRICITY)

SEX APPEAL

SEX APPEAL

*L*et me start by saying that sex appeal is not nearly as important as friendship or respect. The reality is, before we know anything about anyone it is usually all we have to go on. Those physical factors do the talking initially, in most cases. It is important because it does add spark to a relationship. In other words, in our proverbial house of love, sex appeal is the electricity that keeps the excitement alive. Therefore, it has its place as level two in the hierarchy because without it many relationships won't even exist.

Of course, when it comes to the actual, physical act of sex there are certain attributes that spark our interest long before it gets physical. However, "Sex-Appeal" is not about all things sexual. It is by in large about appeal or characteristics that arouse interest. Having said that, I must take a moment and address the physical side of sexuality. Physical attraction holds a hierarchy all its own. There is first an element of fantasy. People tend to have in their minds a preconceived idea of that perfect looking someone. Therefore, how sexy or attractive a person is, depends on how closely they fit the fantasy. That ideal sexiness is an asset to the ego. Having an attractive person to accompany you at any given time makes us look even better. It's true by our own standards and by the world around us too. Second, there needs to be some level of respect. Not at first, but for longevity it must be established. Without it the fire goes out. Third, there needs to be an exchange of consideration, friendship and commitment. If you fail to appeal to someone's softer side you may replace warm thoughts with frustration, anger and resentment. If you want someone to feel like they don't want to live their life without you, be sure not to continually do or say things that make them want to get away from you. Those will add up to "I'd rather do without you" more likely than "I don't want to live without you". Finally, there is physical compatibility. When all things are in place and yet your love life is still suffering, it could be lack of physical compatibility. People often make reference to a good dancer being a good lover. The general idea is to have a partner who can move in sync with you. Someone who moves to the same rhythm and speaks the same body language as you. If one is doing the tango while the other is doing the salsa it is going to be an awkward dance and an unpleasant one at that. Just as in dancing, this is not the time for thinking. Men, be careful not to get so caught up in your performance that your partner feels like she's the background in your solo. Believe me she won't be impressed! This is the time for feeling and sensing. There cannot be a partnership of two followers, neither can there be a partnership of two leaders. Each person may have to follow, lead, teach, learn, slow down and speed up interchangeably and most importantly you have to know when to do what, all by sensing and feeling.

That said, there are many components that contribute to attraction outside of the physical act. Some things are even more sustaining than physical compatibility and good looks. The time does come when we're not so focused on looks. Yes, it is true! That is when you have to be able to shift gears out of the fantasy and into the real…and be valuable there too. Believe it or not, that takes sexy to a new level. In fact, it is those real moments that build respect, friendship and reach a person at a deeper level. It is those things that make us fall in love and want to share our lives with someone. For most women and even some men, especially of a certain age, sex appeal is deeper than physical attributes. Let me rephrase that! When it comes to longevity, that is if you want to be considered, "a keeper", the qualifying components are deeper than the shape of your body or its parts. Sexiness may be one hundred percent about physical attributes at first site but if the personality doesn't fit the look then the fantasy is quickly lost. Ever met an extremely attractive person and then they speak, and their language or conversation quickly makes you change your mind? Even as soon as the first ten minutes we can learn that physical attributes are not enough to hold our interest. It's one of those things that if present, it's holds about ten percent of importance, but if not present, it's about fifty percent or more important.

This chapter is about those things that appeal to us because the more a person appeals to us the more they stay on our mind. Conversely, the more we can appeal to someone the more we stay on their mind. If you want to get someone thinking about you all the time you better learn what appeals to them physically, mentally, spiritually, emotionally, etc. All these aspects of appeal contribute to sex appeal. In order to be sexy and remain sexy you need to know there's more to it than looks.

Physical Attraction

We cannot deny that to most of us, this is a very important trait and it is all right, but thank God that, what is physically attractive means something different according to each individual. Therefore, we do not all need to try to reinvent ourselves to fit one mold. What looks good to one person may not look so good to another. The thing about today's society is if you feel unattractive, you can become very attractive. Even by your own standards because we are our own biggest critic. In addition, those who are very attractive can easily be physically unattractive. In most cases, all we have to do is grow older and become inactive then many of us learn that beauty is fleeting. Although we know that time can turn our prince into a frog we sure do fall in love with gorgeous people, merely because they are gorgeous.

What is it about beautiful people that makes us love them so much that we are willing to except many more unattractive personality traits, than we will of someone that is less attractive to us? For one, I think, besides being fun to look at, the more attractive a person is, the more we feel somewhat validated by our connection to them. It is like the more luxurious our car is the more we are motivated to drive it and show it off. We are willing to pay more for a nice looking lemon than an excellent running ugly vehicle. In many cases, not only does it upgrade our own level of attractiveness, but also it makes a statement that makes others respect, and maybe even envy us. That is in many ways, why we tend to look more towards an attractive appearance because of what the connection will do for our own image. We even say it to each other, "we look so good together". Worse yet we make judgments about couples we do not even know based on appearance. We have all probably done it before. You see an attractive man with a woman you feel is not so attractive and you say, "What is he doing with her?" We also say things like "How did he get her?" When we see an attractive woman with a man we feel is not so attractive, or "He must have a lot of money!" Most of us have been guilty of that at least once. This is a clear indication of just how screwed up we are, not to mention superficial and shallow. I consider myself a leader, so I will be the first to admit, I am guilty as charged! It is almost like a reflex to think that way initially, but thank God, for experience and wisdom that we may learn, not all things pretty are keepsakes! Building a foundation based primarily on physical attraction is the ultimate synthetic connection. It is about as valuable as a big, beautiful, majestic and expensive wedding that precedes a marriage that only lasts several months. We must learn to find that diamond in the rough. Remember we now live in a society that makes being gorgeous a tangible, possibility for us all, so do not discount the value of someone who you may think is physically not your type. If you cannot grow or shrink something with a pill, you can buy something to hold you together, lift you up, or increase you in some way. All that you cannot accomplish with exercise and the proper diet, a surgeon can suck it out, cut it out or add it on. In addition, acne treatments and skin care products are in high demand so they must be working. You get the picture!

My point is to make it clear just how subject to change, physical appearance is. It is highly more likely that your looks will change before your personality does. In some cases, perhaps your looks have gone through quite a few changes in just a couple of years but you still have the same values and goals you have had your entire adult life. Realistically speaking, completely omitting good looks from our criteria list is something most of us are not likely to accomplish. I'm not suggesting that we should. If we are lucky, maturity will get us to a place where a person's appeal is measured by their character traits first and all other attributes are a bonus. We would avoid a lot of agony if we could learn to value people based on what we see on the inside first. Even if you prefer someone who is attractive, a pretty face and a nice body shouldn't be at the top of the requirement list. After all, you may be settling for very little if someone only has to bring good looks to the table. Besides it is a very low set of standards to only require someone to be good looking, after all they are usually not responsible for that. Which means they cannot take credit for it, so when you meet, if they are good looking already, ask yourself, what else can I expect of them? Frankly speaking, it should raise the question, "God did that so now what are you going to do?"

Let me digress for a moment, I do not mean to suggest that beautiful looking people cannot also be genuine and beautiful on the inside as well. That is far from the message I am trying to deliver, especially since I consider myself one of the beautiful people, and I want to go ahead and suggest you adopt the same belief about yourself. That being said, get over yourself! It is not your best asset and it is not all you get to bring to the relationship nor should it be your greatest requirement when looking for a mate. Do not get me wrong, I am still a realist and let us face it physical attraction is powerful. After all, it is all we have to go on in our first impression, in most cases, and in our society, we had better be able to "hold our own" so to speak. It is by in large the source of sex appeal, but if you have standards for what you want someone to look like you better be able to uphold to those same standards yourself and even exceed them. Keep in mind, a person who is physically fit works hard to stay that way. That kind of person probably wants a mate who is physically fit as well. If you are attracted to beautiful smiles you need to make sure your own is beautiful. You need to know that you have to be able to supply that which you demand. We see it all the time where men and women too, have a list of things they think is attractive and yet they don't look like the things on their own list. Imagine that!

Physical attraction is not the "nuts and bolts" of a lasting and loving relationship. I do realize it is not something to be discounted either. Initially, you're going to need something to get his eyes on you and in some cases keep his eyes on you. Good looks act as a sort of surge that gives a relationship a fun energy. However, I contend, its power has its limits, and you might agree if you consider other relationships including some from your past. What do you think you have to offer besides your looks and sexuality? In addition, what do you think you may have lacked in the past that contributed to the demise of the relationship? You should consider these things. Not necessarily to change and do better the next time but to figure out what was it about that person that brought that out of you. On the other hand, what was it about them that did not inspire you to be good to them? This is what I mean about balance. When you find your match, things fit like pieces of a puzzle. Those things that had been lacking in past relationships come easier with a partner that fits you. Your best qualities come out effortlessly. Physical attributes are no longer the main focus. A relationship that works is a thing of beauty.

Synthetic Verses Organic Connections

In this chapter, I want to address the differences between surface feelings verses core feelings. What I mean by surface feelings is when your feelings are developed from superficial factors or unstable factors. One common example is when someone falls in love with a person because they make good money or they are good looking. A person's things can serve as a distraction that takes your focus away from them. However those things make them more attractive to you and those feelings seem very genuine. It can be a lot of pressure on that person to have to continue to live up to those standards in order to hold on to that attention. When you are excited about someone because you're comfortable with them, or enjoy their company this is an organic connection. It eliminates feeling as if we need to be perfect for someone. After all, it is not about being perfect. It is about being perfect for each other. Perfection in this sense is the best fit for you. If you are in tune with your own personality when you meet someone, you feel secure to be yourself. First, you have to love yourself and know who you are. Then when you are comfortable with yourself, it is important to know what kind of personality, in a mate, keeps you balanced. Feeling connected in a relationship also helps you to understand that person even if you do not like the choices they make. Understanding creates empathy and builds friendships.

Sometimes we get to such a place of desperation to find a mate that we cannot tell if there is a true connection or if they are just fulfilling a physical or an emotional void. Therefore, we just go with the flow. One problem could be that some of us do not have enough self-esteem to have any standards at all; therefore, any kind of attention or advances are a plus.

That is an invitation for trouble on so many levels. Even if you do not feel desirable or attractive and you find yourself wondering why nobody would want you, you still deserve to be loved and you should be selective. Now I am not talking to you if you are looking for something to play with. In that case, love is not for you. However, it is my guess that if you are reading this book, this applies to you. There are certain personality traits in a mate that are a comfortable fit for you. I know I made that sound like an old beat up pair of slippers but real love is just that comfortable even when it is rocky. That is organic! Natural just digests easier. You can get comfortable and be yourself for real love.

Then there is the relationship where everything is difficult. You cannot seem to agree on simple things. You choose your words carefully to avoid arguments, or you have to look a certain way all the time or you feel unaccepted. Relationships do require work but it ain't calculus! It is not supposed to be that hard. That is synthetic! I am not discounting the need to add spark and keep your relationship refreshed. I am simply saying that if you are in love with him, he does not have to have a daily ritual to keep you there, and vice versa.

I learned the difference when I was a young girl, just a teenager in fact. You know when you're a young girl your elders love to tell you, "you're young…its just puppy love… you're going to fall in love so many times by the time you grow up". That was not the case. That relationship ended in my early twenties and I got well into my thirties, still looking for love like I knew it as a kid. In my childhood relationship, the external factors paled in comparison to the internal connection I shared with my high school boyfriend. I am still learning from that relationship. It stretched me and shaped me in ways I remain grateful for even though it was turbulent, at best. I used to think it was because I was a child with the impressionable mind of a child, that I was so in love. But the older I got and the more I heard the stories of other women, I learned it was just a rare blessing to learn real love at all, and even more rare to learn so young. I realized how many women never really experienced love and I decided to make it my lot in life, to reach out to as many as will hear me, to help you attain the real thing. The organic connection! It does the heart good; even at its worse, it is better than a synthetic relationship at its absolute best. It may look good and feel good for a while but it withdraws more than it invests and eventually you realize you are still unfulfilled.

Criteria (the checklist)

I believe we fall into this mode when we give up on the belief that there is a person that is right for us. By us, I mean that I too had a checklist. What is this you ask? This is when we decide that we will tolerate a relationship just as long as a person has certain qualities. We may even make the dreaded mistake of marrying someone if they fit a certain criteria. What is wrong with that, you ask? What is wrong with it is that love has nothing to do with this list. I remember thinking at one time that I can't fall in love. I sincerely believed I was incapable. It seemed everyone I met or even dated was just someone to pass the time. I could take them or leave them. I decided that I can't continue to date one man after the next for the rest of my life I have to settle on one, even though I won't love him because I'm incapable of that. I made out a mental list. No, actually I wrote it down on paper. I figured if he fit a certain criteria,

I could tolerate him and be content for life. I thought I was trying to live my life right. I got married to a young man who fit my little list. Yes I said little list because not only did I not believe I could fall in love I also believed most men were idiots by nature so there was no need to require much from him. Talk about shooting yourself in the foot… with that mentality I did just that. As you might imagine, that marriage didn't last very long. I didn't set myself up for fulfillment because I gave up on the real essence of what nurtures a fulfilling relationship—love. Me with my list and my warped views had it all figure out. It doesn't matter if your list is long or short. It could be long as the street you live on, it is not the basis of longevity and certainly not a good foundation for a marriage.

There are many different things couples experience that you couldn't possibly solve with a checklist. That is the basic idea behind the checklist. You thought of many scenarios of past relationships and figured out what has annoyed you most. You then created in your mind, a list of things you feel would neutralize or fix these kinds of problems—Voila! If he has no kids, there will be no baby-mama-drama…if he has money in the bank then maybe he's responsible…blah, blah, blah. I know how it goes I've done it. Let me tell you why it's a bad idea. You cannot possibly know what your needs will be in your future as a couple with that person. Therefore, you cannot possibly premeditate a solution list for future problems. One cookie cutter list does not fit all relationships. First, the two of you have never been a couple before. You don't know what that person will bring out of you or inspire you to feel. Secondly, there are simply going to be some things that have no solution but they are indeed problems and the only thing that will fix them is time. All you can do in the meantime is love each other. If love isn't present, it won't work. Simply put, only genuine love can tolerate certain things. Again, I must give my disclaimer. I'm not suggesting that you shouldn't have standards even if you're in love. It is quite possible that you or the one you love could use a little time to grow, perhaps get your finances right and your lives on track before you commit to marriage and babies. You should most certainly allow time for that! It is extremely important. I assure you, that if you commit to a person based on set criteria because you have convinced yourself you can tolerate it, eventually you'll realize you cannot.

A criteria list to determine if an individual is right for you will not render a solution but a list to quantify the connection between the two of you just may. Take the "four parts of appeal mentioned in the prologue, and think about what character traits define those for you. After you have done that count, how many traits in total there are. Divide that number into 100, whatever number you get rate your current mate on a scale of zero to the number in question. Zero meaning, having no characteristics and the highest number meaning the perfect fit for you. For example, let's say consider our four parts of appeal as they pertain to you. Each bullet represents traits you deem necessary if someone was your friend, if you respect a man/woman, what makes someone sexy, and builds trust according to you. This is an example list:

Friend

- Empathy (person has to be able to relate to you)
- Similarities (things in common)
- Loyalty
- Reliability

Respect

- Leader (have a take-charge attitude)
- Spiritually Grounded
- Ambitious
- Intelligent

Sexy

- Physically Fit
- Beautiful Smile
- Confidence

Trust

- Consistency
- Selflessness
- Honesty

There are fourteen traits in total 100/14=7.14. We'll just make this an even seven. Therefore, each trait is given a scale of (0-7). Rate your mate on how closely he or she may fit your ideal preference in a mate by assigning a number to each of these traits on the scale of (0-7). If your mate gets sevens on all traits then you can quantify that he/she is 100% appealing to you. If you find you are in an unhappy relationship despite that, your problem is probably that what you want is not what you need, or you do not quite know what you want. If your mate is low in some areas and high in others, then you may be able to determine some of the issues in your relationship. You may be able to pinpoint where the strengths and the weaknesses are. Either way, you learn something about yourself and or your relationship. This exercise is better if the two of you do this together.

Two problems with this list are, one; doing this may reveal some truth that you, individually or as a couple may not be prepared to deal with, and two; if you are confused about who you are and what you want in your own life then you may not even be qualified to make such a list. One pre-requisite for this list is that you have graduated with honors from level one. In many cases, simply the process of making the list and thinking about such things might bring some enlightenment. The mere fact that you have actually broken things down and attached a value to it may be awakening in itself.

Passion

Passion is to have deep, emotional feelings about something or someone. Someone who is passionate about their work takes pride in their work and put their best efforts into it. Similarly, someone who is passionate about someone takes great care when dealing with that person. The more two people appeal to one another the deeper the passion between the two. Passion is the spark that keeps the thrill alive. A passionate relationship is the affects of deep-seeded emotions. You cannot achieve passion without reaching someone's emotions. When you think about what people are passionate about, there are multiple emotions involved. People are passionate about things when they enjoy doing them, so there's fun involved. It is usually a stress reliever or an escape for them. Therefore, it is therapeutic. It is usually something that challenges them and yet comes naturally to them. A passionate love life is the by-product of a passionate relationship. Don't expect a dry uneventful, tense relationship to translate as passion in the bedroom. The passion has to be a regular practice in your non-sexual activity before it can flow into the bedroom. Consider the things you are passionate about, your career, your hobbies, now consider why you are so passionate about these things. Your relationship will bring out those same emotions if it were also fun, exciting, therapeutic, challenging and natural. If you are in a relationship or marriage for many years passion may come and go, but if the foundation of your relationship is strong you can always rekindle it.

How To Get The Response And Attention You Want

This subject is a book all by itself but I will touch briefly on some key points. We know there are many sides to our personality. Many attributes make up our collective self. Just as there are many attributes to the sense of self, likewise are there many attributes that appeal to the multiple dimensions of a person. Specific actions render specific responses. I'm sorry I have to keep reiterating that but it is the most important factor of the entire message. If you want someone to respond to you in a certain way, you have to learn to appeal to that side of their personality so they are inspired to respond to you in the manner you'd prefer. Love only seems unconditional because we have already met the conditions of appeal when someone decides they are in love with us.

We often fail to see that the changes we want to see in others have to start within ourselves. You may be able to get someone to do what you ask sometimes simply by asking, but when you want a person to feel something that they do not feel, you have to inspire that. You do not just want someone to show you affection you want them to feel affection for you. *Doing* and *feeling* are as different as being tolerated verses being preferred. So how do you get someone to want you the way you want to be wanted, or treat you the way you want to be treated? The answer is appeal. What is appealing however is different and unique for each individual. It is up to you to learn your love interest's personality and appeal to it. You are not going to get someone to like what you like by forcing things on them. In many situations, people respond to us based on how we communicate with them and others around us. In other words, when people watch us being ourselves they form an opinion of us. The opinions they form guide the way they interact with us. If you want sensitivity, you have to appeal to the sensitive side of a person. If you want sensuality, you have to appeal to the sensual side. If you want to build the friendship, you have to think and behave like a friend, etc...They are not all-in-one, each has a separate set of requirements.

Getting Your Mate To Open Up To You:

If you want someone to open up to you, you have to be approachable, relatable, and somewhat open yourself. Let down your walls if you want to invite them to approach. Do this by engaging in small talk. Sometimes reveal your faults or vulnerabilities. Don't be bossy, judgmental, critical, and do not twist their words to make their comments about you and use that against them. They will shut down on you and close you out. If you are always, right and don't make mistakes it's the same as putting up walls that close people out. Be a good listener. Some people listen and some people wait to speak. If you're not a good listener, you're a bad conversationalist. If you cannot listen because you love to hear yourself speak, you may find you're the only one who does. If you somehow become the victim at the end of every conversation, no one wants to deal with that. A person that's always the victim is just annoying. You may actually make someone avoid you instead of open up to you. You cannot let every conversation affect you. Sometimes you just need to be a listening ear and a good friend. Take yourself out of the situation. Try to see things from their perspective. Don't always give your advice; wait for someone to ask for it sometimes. Nobody likes a know-it-all, especially if you're not stating facts and it is just your strong opinion. In response, it's ok not to have an opinion. You can respond by saying things like; "really?...Why do you feel that way?...and then what happened?"...Just enough to let them know you are listening to encourage them along. Simple responses will make them feel comfortable enough to keep sharing. Finally, if someone is going to tell you their most intimate feelings they need to feel you can keep their secrets. Not use them against them later. Not tell other people. Respect them with a code of confidentiality. How would you want them to react to you in the same situation? These are just some key things to keep in mind if you are trying to encourage someone to share their feelings on a deeper level.

Neutralizing The Arguments

If you find your conversations, tend to lead you into arguments first, you need to know that is not normal. If this is common for you in all your relationships, well then, you need to know…it's you. If this is not a common thing for you, it could be either your mate is an argumentative person, or the two of you just don't understand one another. It is as if you speak two different languages. Its like I said before, understanding makes the relationship go smoother. If you are not connected, a lot can get lost in translation. It is possible there is no harm intended but simple misunderstandings can lead to some big arguments. How do you stop it? My philosophy is; if you want to stop a habit, you starve it. If you feed the argument with more arguing, you're simply adding flames to the fire. Someone has to compose him or herself. It should be you. Lead by example in this situation. If you speak calmly and respectfully, that is avoiding insults and cussing, you set the stage for a calm composed response. If the response escalates to a louder, more agitated tone, remain composed and calm. Don't let it get you too ruffled. You can even say, "I'm not going to argue" and mean it. When the tone escalates, stop talking, and engaging in it, especially if you're being insulted. I know it's hard to do but try the calm composed approach. People don't tend to argue with themselves. You can send a stronger message with actions or the absence of actions than you can with words.

If you engage in certain behaviors, how can anyone assume you don't like that activity? If both of you are shouting no one is listening, then you start hitting below the belt and it only gets worse. If one person is calm, the argument looses half its fuel and has to die out. One way to communicate is by writing to one another. Write your message without insults. Avoid all capital letters because it translates as shouting. Avoid cuss words. If your only motivation for saying, what you have to say is to insult or to hurt, it's not worth communicating it at all. Sometimes two passionate people trying to make a point, turns into a war of words. No one is over talking the other in a note. Every word you are trying to convey is heard. Leave the note in a place your mate can read it in private when the two of you will be apart for some time. Even if the note you receive expresses something, you don't want to hear you have a chance to calm down before the two of you discuss it further. I'm not suggesting that you should reduce your communication to letter writing and avoid conversation altogether. If you write, you may still need to discuss it later. The writing is simply to allow your self to get it all out and be heard. Sometimes you may find you can downsize the message considerably. A great deal of it was emotional and as you write, you may discover you don't have as much to say. You may even discover that writing it out made you feel better and you don't need to give it to anyone after all.

Winning Affection

This is one problem I can honestly say I have never had. Maybe because I'm such a loner I don't require much attention. Maybe I love my alone time so much that I wouldn't notice if someone was avoiding me at times. Whatever the case, I have learned the more you don't need someone's affection the more they want to give it to you. It sounds crazy but it is true. It's due to a combination of things. I have said it many times before; people are attracted to confident people. If you don't extract much from others to be you, people tend to respect you more. Since we live in the real world people are generally attracted to people who look good and smell good. Yeah I know what you might be thinking, "If someone loves you those things shouldn't matter". You are half-right. Your looks alone will not add to or subtract from someone's love for you but I am not talking about love I am talking about affection.

You want to appeal to all the senses. If your breath is bad, you may be loved but you won't get too many kisses, if any. If you don't put much effort into your appearance, you won't be as interesting to look at as someone who puts lots of effort into their appearance? If you are a woman trying to attract a man you have to act like a lady, look like a lady and smell like a lady. Some things are in his nature, you will not change that. It is better for you to accept that and either fall in line or get out of the line. If you are too aggressive and too pushy, you will not attract a masculine, alpha male. A straight man does not want to spend his life with another man. He needs the sensitivity of a woman to balance him. He needs her vulnerability and her softness to remind him that he is a man. If the woman is too aggressive, he will soon feel emasculated by her masculine energy and it will change the dynamics of the relationship. That would not be appealing to either person, trust me!

Likewise, if you are a man trying to attract a feminine woman you have to "man up". Women want masculine men. That does not necessarily mean muscles and a large stature. Although that does help, do not discount it. What it does mean however, is that a woman wants a man who is not too selfish, lazy or afraid to rescue her. Rescue her from anything that weighs heavy on her mind, her heart, her finances, and ultimately her sense of security... We know you're not superman and you cannot save us from everything. It does work in your favor if we see that you genuinely and diligently try it, without complaining and keeping a tally. Women like men to have a sensitive side yet not be too sensitive. That is, he should possess those qualities, but it should not be his dominant quality. Too much sensitivity in a man makes a woman feel like she has to take charge. She looses the essence of her femininity with such a man. She will eventually emasculate him. It will not work in favor of the relationship. Do not equate calm and quiet with sensitivity. They are not the same. A calm and quiet man can exude a very strong masculine energy that women love. He has to be aggressive in his actions, fearless and take charge. These traits speak to a woman's instincts. It is in the woman's nature to be soft and a man's nature to take charge. Somehow, life put us in roles that have not allowed us to respond to those instincts. Those traits are still in us. If we do not operate in the roles that inspire those instincts, they will not flourish. We may need some help to remind ourselves, those characteristics still exist.

If you are a chatterbox and no one can get a word in edgewise, why even bother talking to you. If you are a crybaby or complainer, your very presence may create negative energy and you will be avoided. If you are someone with low self esteem fake it until you get there for real. You cannot be a push over who will take any kind of treatment. If you're not being treated with respect and kindness, cut them off. Make them earn your affection. When someone sits back and watches you being you, you want them to feel a variety of emotions, positive ones preferably. You want them to be impressed and turned-on. Most importantly, you want them to find it a privilege to get close to you. You can't do this if you are someone they don't respect, or if you have things going on that repulse them, annoy them, frustrate or anger them.

You are certainly not going be all these things all the time. However, some of these attributes ought to be who you are everyday, all day. After all, it makes all the difference in the world when you are "being" and not just "doing". Be as appealing as you can be. Be as close to their idea of a "ten" as you can be, and be it at a distance. Be cool. Find yourself something constructive to do. Don't be so available all the time. Give that person a chance to pursue you. Yes, even if it is your spouse. If you think they are not affectionate toward you, there could be one and/or two reasons for that. One, you are doing something that pushes them away. Two, they are preoccupied with something else. Whichever the case you want the attention on you.

Giving someone the space to pursue you does not mean you have to become rude or cantankerous. In fact you should be charming while you give'm some space. You can be good to someone while you get a life. Don't make winning their affection such a full time job. You will be amazed, as soon as you don't need it, their dying to give it to you.

How Do You Become Irreplaceable?

The first thing you need to know; this is not a formula to keep your mate from cheating. I believe promiscuous people who cannot stay faithful are on a constant quest for validation. An insatiable need for an ego boost, says more about what they lack not what you lack. The more you appeal to someone, the more you stay on their mind. The more you are in harmony with them, the more they feel you are an extension of them. That makes life without you unimaginable. After all, the feelings you are trying to inspire are not just about whether or not they want to live with you forever but that they don't want to live without you at any time. Go back to the list of appeal. When it comes to their list what is your score? If it is not that high, don't get angry or defensive. If this is someone, you love and you want to get more from him or her, you need to know what a total package is to them. Otherwise, you are aimlessly shooting at nothing. First, encourage them to be brutally honest with you. Second, thicken your skin, open your mind and take it on the chin. If you score low on their list, take notice of the things they appreciate about you as well as the things they don't like. Ask yourself, "am I ever going to be that person?" More importantly, do you even want to try? You may already know and agree with the things they dislike. Maybe you had not really considered it as a serious issue for them or your relationship. This can be a point of growth in your relationship if you view it objectively. After all, if you are planning to be with someone for life that person should be able to voice any aversions from his/her perspective. It may be a necessary thing, especially if it keeps them from giving you their all. You cannot fault someone for what they feel or do not feel. It should be exposed and dealt with like any other issue in the relationship. It is better to know and have the power to change it than not know and let it grow like a cancer or fester as a silent killer.

You may even learn they do not know what they want or maybe they are shallow and immature and have a very unrealistic list to begin with. Well, you need to know that too. At least you will know it is not necessarily you. It is just bad timing. If someone is still trying to find him or herself, what is valuable to them is ever evolving. Their expectations can be silly and unrealistic to you if you are more mature than they are because they may not see things the way you do. If the person is emotionally immature, they are motivated by more immediate needs. It is all about what they think they want today, tomorrow it may be different. That being said you cannot change them but you can change you. If you are in a relationship with someone who is immature, you are going to have to allow them to grow. If you know that is you, then you have to figure out what you need to do to develop your full potential and occupy your time doing that individually. It will help you and your relationship for you to grow. Pursue some individual activities. Earlier when I said if you keep finding yourself in a relationship that doesn't fit then you don't know your size. I meant you have to know who you are before you can determine what attributes make up the "full package" for you.

I could go on with many different scenarios but the general principal is still the same. If you are trying to appeal to someone in one way or another, you need to know their specific taste, their mannerism and their communication style. Whether you are trying to encourage or neutralize a certain behavior, you have to bear the burden of change. You cannot appeal to them on your terms. If you were a shoemaker and you want to draw in a clientele of women, maybe a certain age group or a certain class of women, you would definitely study your market and learn their taste. A smart businessperson knows the success of the business depends on how well you do your homework. You have to design specifically to meet the demand. Of course, it's your brand and your esthetic. The key is, you have to learn to do you, but for the customer. When it comes to meeting the demand, it's all about finding the need and filling it. This doesn't mean you have to be someone you're not. I never want you to compromise the essence of you. This is about learning to refine and customize according to the order you're trying to fill.

Level Three
(THE SUPPORT)

FRIENDSHIP

FRIENDSHIP

In my opinion, friendship is the glue that sustains all romantic relationships. In our house of love, friendship is the support beams. It aids the foundation in the stabilization of the building. When all else is worn out or you need to update some things the support beams will still be holding up the building. Friendship is highly valuable. Some may have arguments against this theory but in my opinion, a life-long partnership has to include a solid friendship.

Friends understand each other. Friends hang out with one another simply because they want to. You don't do things for or with your friend because you are obligated. Your friend is your confidant, your buddy, and your shoulder to lean on. You tell your friends things out of love, even if they won't like what you have to say, because you believe you're looking out for them. Most couples who have been married for ten, twenty, and even up to fifty years have had moments when they did not like their mate. At times, a wife can be so mad at her husband she may not want to utter a word to him for days. A husband may even get so tired of the responsibilities of the household that he might feel like giving up and going into early retirement. Yes, even in those marriages that last for fifty years these things are possible. By the time, a couple has reached twenty and fifty years of marriage, they have been through the wringer together. Somebody had to forgive the unthinkable. Somebody had to carry all the weight and the responsibilities for everyone in the family for a while. Somebody felt taken for granted for a while. Many marriages last because the friendship sustains it. The point is, you won't give up on you're best friend. You just can't imagine your life without them. Good or bad, you understand them. Sometimes your mate is not so sexy to you. Sometimes sexiness is not a concern at all. Sometimes life has taken the two of you through so much that you know that person in every kind scenario imaginable and that electricity that new relationships experience is not there. Maybe when the two of you met, you both had a decent income and you were able to go out all the time. You probably had fun shopping and dining out a few days a week. When you decide to marry and start a family priorities change, sometimes life brings unforeseen changes. There may come a time when you cannot make ends meet. The activities you used to have are no longer in the budget. This is when your relationship is tested. Friendship gets you through these times. Friendship helps the relationship evolve into something deeper than the superficial factors that help new relationships thrive. It helps sustain the bond until life turns a corner. Life is full of changes and relationships go through many phases. The friendship keeps the bond strong and pliable enough to move through the vicissitudes of life so you can still come out with a partner. I urge you, not to disregard the importance of the friendship in you relationship. The components within this level of the hierarchy help strengthen the bonds of friendship.

Chemistry

Meaning: "The spontaneous reaction of two people to each other, especially a mutual sense of attraction or understanding." The key word here is "mutual", which means to have the same relation toward each other; held in common; shared. You get the picture. I do not mean to imply that you may not know the definition of chemistry but a clear concise definition may help to show a clearer point of view. This is an ideal component in every kind of relationship. That is why I thought chemistry qualifies as a component in the friend level. Rather the relationship is coworker, friend, sister, or love interest good chemistry just makes the relationship easier. The two substances marry organically. The most electrifying relationship is when two people have a level of chemistry so ideal to one another that they connect almost instantaneously. Chemistry doesn't need much shaking or stirring to mix. The level of intensity goes from zero to one-hundred with little effort. By "shaking and stirring" I mean, the level of work that it takes to become comfortable with one another. This is ideal and rare, but attainable. In addition, while that is a precious commodity in any relationship so blessed to possess it, commitment is required for longevity. You must know what is rare will not come frequently so it behooves you to commit to working on it. It is my belief that this is more attainable for two people who are completely secure in themselves. That is why it is rare. So many people are insecure and unhappy with themselves that a truly, secure, happy person has a hard time finding another secure, happy person.

In many new relationships, there is a certain level of excitement verses a certain level of uncertainty. The more connected you begin to feel to one another the less uncertainty there is. Chemistry between two people enhances the feeling of absolute certainty from the beginning. In other words the more two people can relate to one another the better the chance of them establishing a strong connection. The relationship feels balanced. It is a natural process to pursue balance. The earth it self is on a constant quest for balance. When extreme temperature differences collide, a storm occurs in an effort to balance the atmosphere. When two extremely different personalities try to form a romantic relationship there will be constant storms. The extreme differences will pull each person so far from their personal center that they will fight to feel balanced. We have been told, "opposites attract" for so long that we do not know where to draw the line. Let me be the first to rephrase that. Differences attract, that is variation, not opposite! The root word of opposition is opposite... that is certainly not the idea of a partnership.

Someone completely opposite of you may be too different for you to relate to them. If the two of you don't speak the same language or have the same cues, you'll spend more time misinterpreting each other than anything. When you meet someone with whom you don't have to compromise your personality, you feel a sense of comfort. You are more comfortable with yourself, and in turn, much more comfortable with them. As I said before the intensity goes from zero to one hundred without any effort. You may not even remember the defining moment when you decided, you have met the love of your life. It just goes from one day you met a stranger to; the next day you cannot imagine life without one another. Remember this should be mutual otherwise, that is not chemistry. There is nothing ideal about being at this level of intensity alone. That would be a disastrous situation, which is quite the opposite of the picture I'm trying to paint for you.

In fact, I have said many times that a relationship is stronger when both people have a strong sense of self. I'm going to give you a scenario to paint a clearer picture as to why this is so important. Ann; is a person whose confident and comfortable with herself. She has a tendency to be very content when she's alone. Her personal time is important to her. She tends not to take other's actions personal so she's not easily ruffled. She is quite a bit laid back in many situations where others may be emotionally reactive. When paired with someone who is considerably less self-assured. Bob, who may not particularly like being alone, Ann's love of alone time, translates to Bob as avoidance. Ann is understanding of personal time, therefore doesn't mind and even encourages Bob to hang out with friends and find some activities. This feels to Bob like she's pushing him away or trying to get rid of him. He may even believe Ann has someone else she likes better.

On the other hand, when Ann is going out with friends or out alone, Bob is always angry, envious or suspicious though Ann may be innocent. Bob may even develop a defensive personality toward Ann to sort of rebel against his constant desire to be close to her. In his mind, Ann is being insensitive to his feelings and since he can't get what he wants out of her he withholds certain acts of kindness and affection. He may not compliment her even when he really wants to. He may try to avoid her to give her a taste of what he feels. In Bob's mind, he is going to be tougher. This is yet another tactic to get a rise out of Ann. When his efforts don't render him desirable, results he's more frustrated and blames Ann for that too. Ann, at this point feels like Bob just has a bad attitude all the time. She doesn't quite get what his problem is. In this kind of situation Ann's laidback demeanor is always misread as uncaring, nonchalant, or even unfaithful in the eyes of Bob.

According to Ann, Bob should relax, get some hobbies or find some friends. In many cases, Bob may resort to all kinds of shenanigans just trying to get a rise out of Ann. To Bob, calm, composed and laid back is just Ann's way of withholding affection. It's wearing thin for Ann and it is pushing her further away. The two are constantly at odds because they are in fact an odd couple. Their life together is a constant battle of miscommunication and misunderstandings. The problem is the two are mismatched, or shall I say too opposite. Ann frequently has to apologize just for being her self, which keeps her, frustrated. Bob is always suspicious and feeling unappreciated which keeps him angry with Ann and often feeling insecure. They are both good people and are generally good to one another but they cannot relate to one another. The relationship is always tense and it feels like hard work all the time. This is an exhausting situation. People do however live in this predicament for many years because they cling to hope because their mate is a good person. Each one may be the nicest or most responsible person the other has ever dated. They cannot figure out why they just cannot live in peace with each other. Each feels constantly, wrongfully accused, taken for granted, and misunderstood. If this is your life and you want to make this work, it's going to take a lot of "just getting over it". It is certainly not personal and there is probably no malicious intent on either part.

Ann is not likely to give up her alone time because she thrives from it. It is her time to collect and unwind. It is where she finds her center. She is not likely to develop the excitable cheerleading demeanor Bob craves. Bob is not likely to relate to Ann anytime soon because it is a growing process and he's just not there yet. Frankly, many adults have not reached that level of growth. Good luck and be patient!

Sometimes we are blessed enough to meet someone that just makes being ourselves a lot easier. It's not that we've had to be fake all the while before meeting them but what it really is; some people make simple things difficult. In an effort to live peaceably among one another we make adjustments, constantly. In some cases we have made adjustments for so long, we've lost a bit of ourselves over time. Perhaps you've become a bitter person, or quick tempered. Maybe you've become guarded and mistrusting. You may even be thinking, "I have not always been like this!" When you have chemistry with someone, you may not remember the defining moment for the bliss you suddenly feel. When you try to process what was wrong in your former relationships you may not remember the defining moment that turned you from a person at peace to some one with no tolerance at all.

If your life puts you in one situation after the next where you're making personality adjustments, well, you've quite possibly lost yourself many times over. You may not even know what you prefer anymore. Then you meet that someone that helps you find you. With little effort, your personalities fit just like the pieces of a puzzle. We like to say opposites attract yet we look for things we have in common. When the connection is right, we get enough of both. It is all about balance. Where it matters most, there is not too much of anything or too little, it is just the right amount. The outcome is a harmonious marriage of two personalities.

This is so ideal that I'm going to go out on a limb and say, except nothing less! That is, if you've had enough of just being with someone to keep you company. Your bad relationships can serve as a benefit to help you recognize and appreciate the right person when you meet them as long as you don't jump into one relationship to get over another. Once you've had enough bad relationships to compare a good one to, you can better appreciate it. Hopefully you won't be fooled into thinking you'll fall in love again and again, like your elders used to tell you. That kind of thinking may cause you to make decisions you'll later regret. Good chemistry is not easily found. If it is a loving relationship you want you must have good chemistry with that person otherwise it's more work than it's worth. A relationship with great chemistry is just easier to be in. I like to say it's like blinking or breathing. You don't even think about the process you just live it. Even in such a relationship there will be challenges, that is the nature of relationships and life itself. However, the burden is lighter, the process is easier, and the recovery is faster.

If you're wondering how you will know if there's chemistry between the two of you, that's just it, you won't have to wonder. You'll find yourself communicating in ways you haven't in other relationships. You'll discover that even disagreeing isn't as bad as with others. The most important thing you will discover is that no matter what happens you won't love him today, hate him tomorrow, and then love again. No matter how mad he makes you, you'll always be able to say, without a doubt, "I still love him".

I know many women go back and forth in and out of love with the same person. Depending on how good things are between them this month or week, she's in love and next week she's calling him a bunch of names and talking about his kids and his mama. That is something! I just wouldn't say it's love. The truth is, if the pattern of your time spent together, is repeatedly good this week and bad next week let it go! Don't try to hold on to something like this by fooling yourself into believing that you're going to go through something like this with everyone you meet. If you do in fact go through this with everyone you meet you need to take self-inventory. You are part of the problem. Don't convince yourself that it's not all bad. While it is true, you are going to go through something in every relationship, you're not going to go through it that frequently if that person is right for you. Furthermore if you find yourself saying "it ain't all bad" too frequently, it probably is. My guess is, you're trying to talk yourself out of thinking, its not good enough to keep. Well it isn't! Trying to hold on to something that is causing you more frustration, pain or sorrow than joy and fulfillment is just not worth the headache or the precious time you're losing. Your relationship should not be like an ongoing homework assignment. That is not the idea behind the phrase, "relationships take work".

Cohesiveness

To make a relationship work you are going to have to compromise some things cohesiveness is about working together. This is not always easy. Unlike chemistry, this is a choice. You can make a conscience decision to live in cooperation with someone. For example, each individual uses what he/she is strongest in or better at for the good of the overall unit, the family, or the relationship. Your gifts are not yours to keep for yourself. Keep in mind, when you give your best you inspire others to provide their best to support you in your areas of weakness. This is how two people can achieve success in multiple areas as a couple.

If you want to add years to the life of the relationship, you must be committed to common goals. You need to be able to work together in many different situations and you need to maintain the loyalty to one another, even when you disagree. This is why cohesiveness is important. Cohesion promotes trust and fosters partnership. It is important to stay committed and work in cooperation with your mate in spite of your mood. It will earn your mates respect and loyalty and strengthen the bond between you.

Empathy

Empathy is not to be confused with sympathy, which is slightly different by definition. The act of being empathetic is being able to share in someone's thoughts and feelings and connect to their situation. Having sympathy is more of a feeling of pity or feeling sorry for someone. Empathy is when you put yourself in someone's shoes so to speak. Empathy is a good thing to have in a relationship of any kind. Empathy helps to drive concern and consideration. It supports loyalty and friendship. To be empathetic is to try to relate to your mate. This is how you appeal to the softer side of someone. Sometimes we need to respond empathetically to a situation. It eliminates the self –righteousness, and the victim mentality. It helps you to be a more understanding person. Understanding goes a long way. Sometimes parents are more lenient with their own children than with someone else's children simply because they understand their own children's motives, even when they don't like the behavior. The mere fact of knowing or understanding what led someone to do what they did inspires empathy. Empathy for one another will help you support each other even in your differences. If you can be more empathetic toward your mate, you may open him up in ways he had not opened up before.

If you find you are not empathetic in your relationships you need to evaluate that relationship or yourself. Whether it is a platonic friendship, intimate relationship, parent and child, or even business partners, you should be able to empathize with that person from time to time. Empathy is the emotion that separates the sociopaths from the non-sociopaths. It is a quality most of us have. It is a good characteristic to replace anger...at least on occasion. Empathy is one of the most important emotions humans possess to keep us humble and connected. With all that said, it is not only a good thing to have in any relationship, it is essential to the bonds of friendship.

Nonsexual Intimacy

For many people intimacy is synonymous with sex. Intimacy is the prerequisite of romantic sex but it is not the definition of sex. It is about being close, familiar, and personal but it is a bad policy to turn every act of closeness into a sexual encounter. Better yet, I should say it is a bad policy if you cannot be close unless it leads to sex. Nonsexual intimacy contributes to other components necessary in the four parts of appeal. For instance the friendship, friends can be close without the need for erotic pleasure. The friendship zone of your relationship needs intimacy and you should be able to get close without the need for a happy-ending. You should be able to do things like cook together or play games together.

It promotes good feelings about one another in other ways that are important to building the bond. In the long run, the sexual part of the relationship may change. None of us know what kind of deficiencies growing older may bring. I'm not talking about being elderly I'm talking as early as late thirties and early forties. Hormones, body image, vitality... just to name a few, can all become not quiet as efficient as they used to be. In that case, what will you have? Practice some other feel good activities that encourage laughter, fun, excitement and relaxation between the two of you. It can build trust when someone feels you want to be close to them just because, and they feel it is safe to let down their guards. It is important to try to build a well-rounded relationship. It makes the bond stronger and longevity a more likely outcome.

Nurturing

To nurture something is to encourage it to flourish. Love needs encouragement. You have to put in the time, make the commitment and even make some sacrifices if it is going to grow. That does not mean that you have to be overly accommodating or uncharacteristically nice. That might be a turn-off and might translate as insecure or overbearing. The goal is to be attentive not annoying. People have individual preferences and needs. To encourage growth you have to supply what is essential to the person whose love you want to encourage. What is his/her deal breaker, or bottom line. What is his/her turn offs and likewise what turns him/her on. That is not necessarily a reference to sex but merely an indication of what evokes positive and negative emotions in the person you are trying to impress.

Have you ever met anyone who meets your needs without asking you anything? They just see your needs and fill them. That kind of person makes you feel like they don't mind doing anything for you. In turn, it inspires you to support them in any situation as well. It just makes you all warm and fuzzy! Then there's the other kind of person that you find yourself doing all kinds of things for, yet, when you need them the most, they are MIA. That kind of person makes you slowly separate yourself. They are clearly not team players. You don't want to be that person if you are trying to improve closeness. If you want the relationship to move in your favor, you have to be a good partner. If you love someone, you'll have his back. Reserving your best resources for yourself will keep you from forming a partnership. It is especially frowned upon when your love one needs you most. I know there are some that will give anyone anything. I'm not suggesting you should relinquish your bank account and your credit cards and the keys to your car for someone you just met. If you are doing that...Stop It! That is buying affection and you will never know love if you think that you have to buy it. Furthermore, you will be misused and possibly end up with nothing. I mean for those of you who are in a healthy relationship with someone you love and trust and that person also loves you. The relationship will not flourish if you are selfish. To nurture the relationship both individuals need to invest in it. You have to invest your heart, your time, your money and your energy to help it flourish. Just as sure as time changes, you both will change. Learn to be selfless. Love may get inconvenient, plan ahead.

Level Four
(THE SECURITY)

TRUST

TRUST

Trust is not just about whether you believe you have a cheating mate, although that is very important. Trust in this context is about credibility. It is also about whether or not you feel your mate is reliable and has your best interest at heart. It is even about how much you feel he is capable of thinking of others' well-being such as your children from another relationship or marriage, your elderly parents or grandparents, etc. Remember when you enter into a marriage, your spouse is not only your family but also your family's family as well. Essentially, it comes down to rather or not you can trust your mate's decisions, opinions, judgment and leadership. After all, what we all really want is a loving relationship with a partner for life. The operative word is partner. I find that couples don't share their finances when they don't trust their mate's money management habits. Couples who are together but separate live like roommates. This occurs because people feel like they may somehow sacrifice their own security if they relinquish all. We are so afraid of the possible break-up taking us for everything that we end up making it a reality. If you have doubts about building your life with someone, you will stunt the growth of your lives together. You have to show commitment to the union. It is bigger than just the two of you. The two of you are the foundation of the unit at large. More so if there are children involved. In Mark 3:24-26 NIV, it states," if a house is divided against itself, that house cannot stand." Even if you don't believe the scripture, you have to admit it makes sense. When it comes to relationships especially when you want to sustain one for life, having trust is necessary. Since we know we can only control our own actions, take action. You have to be trust worthy.

For a woman it is fulfilling to be with a man who inspires her and whose opinion she values, and whose judgment she can trust. Similarly, it is fulfilling to be with someone whose lead she wants to follow. In our society, the concept of a woman following a man's lead has taken on a negative connotation. Women are far removed from the era when male dominance was encouraged and celebrated. This is not about dominance or subservience but it is about support. Having someone to take on the battles of life with you can take a lot of burden off one person. After all, we are created to support, help and balance each other. Men are physically stronger, women are naturally softer, more nurturing. To bring balance we do need each other's support.

I myself have been resistant to follow any man. For the most part, I felt most men couldn't think their own way out of a paper bag even if you left it open for them. To follow that, I thought, would make me the idiot. I'm speaking to the head strong, resilient women when I say this; it is ok to be led. Uplifting even! You may get the sense that you are sort of giving up something if you adopt this kind of thinking. That could be the case but who said this is a bad thing? Maybe the thing you would be giving up has been to heavy for you to carry all along but you've carried it for so long you thought it was the way things are supposed to be. What I mean to say is this, if you meet a man who you admire, intelligent, charming, thoughtful, caring, a man of integrity, and he has the audacity to be good looking and successful on top of it all, you may then allow your mind to entertain the thought that it is highly possible, you and that man can become an item. Following his lead will not be so much a choice as it will be a desire. There lies the difference between the burden of following his lead or the fulfillment in following his lead. First, you have to see him as an honorable person worthy of admiration. That is not something you can fake, and it isn't something you can teach him. He has to be equipped with the attributes that foster that kind of emotion. You should not have to bring it out of him, but it is he, that would bring it out of you.

I do believe that it is a man's lot in life to take the heavy weights. He is built for it. Let that man be a man. I say that with a bit of sarcasm because if he is the right man you do not have to let him be anything, for a true leader will always inspire a following. The point of it all, is that there is a big difference between the kind of emotions that a reverent love brings out of a woman verses an irreverent love. It is in fact, even for the strongest woman a very rejuvenating feeling to meet someone you can love that way. Someone you can trust with your life. Does that make you more vulnerable and more subject to heartache? Possibly! However, I have learned that the greater the risk of your investment the greater the possible return. I guess it just comes down to whether you are content with mediocrity or prefer to build something more enriching. Most importantly, if it's worth having it is worth investing in it. If you are too guarded you will restrict what you give as well as what you receive. You will play an integral part in keeping the relationship from growing.

Compromise

Compromise is about reciprocity and support. It is a natural component of trust. Willingly making personal sacrifices to support your mate's needs, ambitions, and goals is a contribution to the security of the relationship. Many people have ridiculous ideas about the level of sacrifice their spouse or mate should make for them. There may come a time when life knocks the wind out of you and you may need someone to hold you up. You may need someone to hold you together but that should be an isolated incident. Reciprocal compromise and sacrifice strengthens a bond. Don't forget, your mate is human. No matter how strong a person may seem, anyone can get tired. Everyone deserves to be vulnerable sometimes. Anyone can feel overwhelmed at times. These are the times when a person deserves a break. Step in and help. Lighten the load. It is now your turn to be strong and make a sacrifice for them. No one has the right to hold a permanent position as a victim in the relationship just as no one deserves to hold all the weight all the time.

When your partner in life gets overwhelmed, allow him/her a moment of down time. Don't turn the situation around and make it about you. Just because a man is a man, and he may be the breadwinner, does not mean his woman cannot help him in that area so he doesn't get overwhelmed. He may need a break from the stress that comes with that responsibility sometimes. Likewise, just because a woman is the one who bears the children, doesn't mean she has the greater responsibility of caring for the children and the man of the house gets to put that responsibility all on her. A man should routinely cook, clean and interact with his children daily just as she does. I know from experience the both roles carry a load of responsibility. So much so that trying to be good in one role can rob a person of the energy to do anything else. A system of reciprocity balances the weight so no one gets too overwhelmed or feels taken for granted. It is your job to make sure you are as much support in the relationship as you expect to receive. That does not mean that you give a gift in exchange for a gift. What it does mean is everyone has their strengths, something they are good at doing, be sure you invests yours in the relationship. If you feel you can count on your mate to carry some of the responsibilities then I am sure that offers you some level of security. Are you making them feel equally secure? Each one should make an equal investment in the relationship, not identical but equal. Contribute your assets just as you expect it.

Remember life takes quick turns. My former pastor used to say, "Life is full of swift transition" that statement has always resonated with me because it is so true. Don't get complacent in your "role" in your relationship because tomorrow you may be required to change positions. If you want to keep your bond strong, you have to remain pliable. You have to be willing to fill in where needed. Be sure that life will shift. The situation as you know it will change over time and you will need to readjust, perhaps multiple times. That is what relationships are about. Flexibility and selflessness fosters a system of reciprocity. If you can adopt a system of compromise, your relationship is well on its way to happily ever after.

Consideration and Concern

Showing concern and consideration for someone, builds trust. It says you are compassionate and therefore trustworthy. Here is one way to earn a warm-n-fuzzy spot in someone's heart. However, rules do apply. Of course we need this in every relationship. It's worth mentioning because sometimes what we think is considerate may not translate as such to the person we claim to be concerned about. It is really a matter of whether or not you know how to love that particular person. Just as people are different, the way in which you love them should be custom fit for them. Example; maybe your significant other is a quiet, laid back kind of person. Let's say your mate appreciates small gatherings and simple dinners rather than a big parties and lots of attention. You on the other hand can't understand that. In your mind, who doesn't love to be the center of attention? Who doesn't want to be showered with attention by as many people as one building can hold? In this case your mate wants a quiet little dinner for his/her birthday but you spend thousands on a surprise party. Perhaps you even hired some celebrity talent. You had the food catered by a well-known caterer in town, which is hard to book. You spent a lot of time effort and money to put it all together. You say to yourself, (hypothetically speaking) "Toni is going to be so happy on the big day". The day of the party Toni is not happy in fact Toni is a little p'd off because it was clearly stated to you that Toni really wanted a quiet dinner with you and now there's all these people to entertain and he will not get your undivided attention. To Toni, the day would've been more special if you had just honored the request. This kind of thing does happen. Not specifically the big party thing of course! Oddly enough after such a misunderstanding, the gift giver is then upset because they feel unappreciated. It is really just a matter of loving someone the way they need to be loved and not about what you think is better. We're always hearing that we should treat others the way we want to be treated. We need to be generally empathetic to their wishes as we would want them to be considerate of our wishes. The deed is only relevant if it is valuable to the person for whom it was intended. You cannot satisfy someone's cake craving with a really big cookie. No matter how big the cookie, or how many similarities you find they have.

Contractual Agreement

This is the kind of relationship that is built solely on trust. This relationship is when two people connect because of their values in religion, work ethics, social status...etc. Whatever the reason, love has nothing to do with it. The contract is really a rule of roles. This is not necessarily a written or even spoken contract, though anything is possible. It is an unspoken agreement of role responsibility. In this kind of relationship the parties involved have not necessarily given up on passion but have decided that practicality, status, and/or purpose is perhaps more important in life and in a relationship. This relationship is completely reliant on trust. Both parties have made a cognitive commitment to do their part. This kind of union is one of sacrifice.

Unfortunately, this becomes the fate of many relationships. A couple who has been together for many years may have started out very passionate. Then down the line, they build a very comfortable life around their existence together so they just hold on. Some people start out knowing they do not have a passionate, romantic kind of love. They sustain a relationship, and even enter into marriage based on teamwork. I don't think it's a bad thing—If it works for them, God bless them! I do however; think this takes some serious discipline and a very high level of commitment to the cause. It seems more feasible for an elderly couple who marries for companionship and the benefits of shared resources. A younger couple has to be very dedicated to the commitment of the relationship. Younger people have to fight to stay strong enough to resist emotions influenced by outside sources. A contractual relationship is one of responsibility, not in the sense that there is no joy in it but that the bottom line is; a lack of pleasure will not be a deal breaker. In other words, this kind of couple may try to improve the passion. They may have date nights. They may be good friends but they have decided on purpose as their bottom line, not passion. I know it sounds cold and unappealing but it is worth mentioning because it does exist. We all see many "power" couples that appear to have it all because together they have produced so much. You can best believe there was a lot of sacrifice there. One or both parties have taken on a lot, have denied themselves a lot, and have invested a great deal of their time and resources to that union, even if there were times when it seemed it would render them nothing in return.

Many people envy this without taking into account the work involved. It may appear to be a perfect union, but it is only for people disciplined enough to deny themselves emotional satisfaction. That rules most of us out. When things are not feeling good it is difficult to maintain a role that lacks an emotional connection. I am inclined to believe that the people in these relationships have convinced themselves that the things they accomplish together makes up for the lack of passion and romance but are secretly very unhappy.

A commitment to responsibility is an important thing to have in a relationship and it certainly can help make a couple a power couple in many ways. Having a sense of purpose is indeed an admirable trait, but it alone does not build a house of love. It is merely creating structure by setting goals, making plans and then sticking to those plans. A contractual relationship is not for the highly emotional type. A person who thrives from passion and excitement cannot sustain this kind of union. A relationship based on the promise of power or prosperity, will not satisfy emotional needs. Eventually the heart will speak and those emotions will take over. You will feel trapped and anxious to escape. Find your balance. Do not covet the relationship someone else appears to have. It may work for them but not necessarily for you. In fact, it may not really be working for them. They may be good at keeping a united front. Know who you are and you will find what you need.

Level Five
(THE WOW FACTOR)

RESPECT

RESPECT

$\mathcal{R}$espect is important because in the big picture, it contributes to sexual attraction rather we realize it or not. The level of respect a person holds for their mate will determine loyalty, sex appeal and even trust. Therefore, it is not something to overlook. Respect is all about showing honor and consideration. The thing to remember about respect is the most important person in any equation is you. You first have to respect yourself in any relationship because your self-respect will earn you further respect. Consider the image others have of you. Honor yourself by not compromising yourself to win favor. Within a brief moment of meeting someone, we can determine whether or not we think they are educated, ignorant, sophisticated, rude etc. As we get to know someone further and more of their personality is exposed they either confirm our initial observations or defy them. The way you dress, the way you speak, the language you use and the way you treat others, all work together to portray an image of you to the world around you.

For example ladies, you feel neglected by your man and you want to make him jealous. You put on that outfit that leaves nothing to the imagination and go out with the girls.

Yes, you might succeed at getting his attention and making him jealous. Ponder this, what if he looses respect for you because he thinks you're a slacker? What if he thinks you're a bit immature? What if he already thinks you dress too trashy and it embarrasses him? If either of these are the case you will have confirmed his already negative image of you. Having any of those characteristics says you are too unsure of yourself. That makes you a risk and too unstable to invest in. Men are territorial you know? They want to believe what they have is special and not anybody can have it. That is what makes you valuable. You have to know who you are and know your worth. Don't compromise your dignity to get anyone's attention, not even his—He will respect you for it. That is understandable because women want the same thing. We want a strong, confident, attractive man who is selective when it comes to the woman he chooses. The fact that he is selective says to others, he already has his queen. It is a source of pride for us when our mate carries themselves with dignity and respect. We want other people to want what we have but not qualify to get it. Now think about that for a minute. If you must go out sexy do it tastefully. The point is; it is not enough to earn someone's affection and attention if you don't earn their respect.

When it comes to respect we usually think about it in terms of how we want to be treated. I don't think many of us think about whether or not we conduct ourselves in a way that inspires people to respect us. A better way to handle that situation would be to show him you have a life outside of him. You can look your best, do your hair, and have on some sexy shoes, if you want, but do something that wows him. You will definitely get his attention if he sees his beautiful queen on a powerful mission without his input. At the very least, show him that his response to you does not determine your total happiness. Operate with some dignity and self-respect be proud of yourself. In turn, you will become much more valuable to him. You become a sexy powerhouse he cannot afford to lose. In many cases, earning respect is to project a respectful image of your self. In other cases, earning respect is not to accept anything less.

Self-respect is a characteristic that says to others, "I love me. I can and will take care of myself. I'm valuable and worthy of great things and I must be honored accordingly". When someone can pick up those vibes from you, they approach you with respect and they continue to deal with you respectfully.

Reverence

To reverence is to have a deep respect for, or to be impressed with, or in awe of. In reference to a woman toward her man, reverence can also foster submission or the desire to stand by her man against the odds. It most certainly adds to sex appeal and it builds trust. Reverence, in this context is a separate entity from respect. It's respect with something extra. I separated it from respect to highlight how important it is for a woman to revere her man. I don't mean reverence to the extent of bowing down to him in worship. No, that level of reverence belongs only to God and you must be careful not to put any man on that pedestal. I mean she needs to be in "awe" of him, impressed by him. This is important! It has a huge effect on how a woman will respond to him. If he operates in leadership, she will naturally follow. If he has goals and well thought out plans to accomplish those goals she will feel safe with him and support him fully. If he is competent and confident, he will arouse her. If he is compassionate and considerate he will always have her heart. I find this to be true for many women. This may be the section of the book that is most important for men to know.

I consider myself a strong woman. I'm very much a leader and not easily impressed. I like to make my own money and I have my own goals and ambitions. I have a very strong personality, I am intrinsically motivated, and I intend to remain that way. However, even I like to know that when I am with a man I can sometimes be vulnerable. I like to feel like I don't always have to have it all figured out. A woman wants to maintain her right to make decisions and hold the torch at her own discretion. She doesn't want the responsibility of having to do it for the entire family all the time. It is nice for a woman to feel like her man wants to save her. It's even better when she believes he really can. That is the biggest reason why a woman prefers to be with a man who is taller and bigger than she is. She needs to feel delicate and feminine by comparison to her man. The opposite of that scenario, (if he is shorter and smaller) conflicts psychologically with her self-image and affects her role in that relationship. It is a very attractive trait when a woman has reverence for a man. Its holds more weight than a nice car, nice clothes or any cologne he could find. If she reveres him, no matter what changes life may take him through, the world could see him as a bum she will still regard him as a winner. All superficial impressions will dissipate. Simply because he brings out something in her that makes her feel good about being his a woman.

That being said, I find that many young men and sadly some not so young, rob themselves of a fulfilling relationship with a woman. They are afraid they will give too much. They allow the strong woman in their lives to take the lead in most areas. She has to work to contribute to the household (which is fine especially in this economy) but she also has to raise the children with little to no input from him. All or most the financial decisions (burdens) are on her shoulders and she still has to maintain some level of softness to keep the man/women relationship in balance. The woman's softness verses the man's strength is the contrast that keeps this in balance. When he puts her in the position of dominance so frequently, he's slowly robbing her and himself of her softer side. She slowly becomes less vulnerable. Having to bear the mental strain of holding it all together for the family and business, strengthens the woman's resilience and sense of dominance. This is a good thing for her if she's single. It's even necessary. Nevertheless, when she is in a relationship a woman needs to see her man far more resilient and in control than she. When she does not, this works against him because then she won't be a submissive wife. She has too much on her plate. It is far too much too juggle when she has to teeter back and forth from dominant to submissive. She cannot juggle all these responsibilities and interchange personalities as well. It is most likely not going to happen. What will happen is that, while she may love him she's not that attracted to him. She may begin to feel, very unfulfilled as a woman.

Men often mistake this for sexual dissatisfaction because it may affect the woman's sexual desires toward him. Each woman has her own idea of what defines a man. The character traits that she equates with manhood are individual. No matter what they are for that woman, it is in the man's best interest to fit the mold because in the end it is a win, win situation when she respects him as a man. If he's doing things right, there's almost nothing she won't do for him. His efforts will be like making an investment with unyielding returns. The gift keeps on giving! In him, she sees her rock, her other half. According to her, he represents her well and she's proud to be a reflection of him.

However, you should adhere to the concept mentioned in level one. It is always most important to have your own self-image and self-esteem in tact. You should love yourself first. That is for sure! Then you'll be able to develop a genuine love for someone else and respect for them based on realistic capabilities. If you do not come into the relationship with those priorities in tact the reverence you have for him will be more like a form of worship, which can, and will, eventually backfire on you. You see you must first, have God in his proper place as head of all things. Secondly, you must have a great deal of love and respect for yourself and your own capabilities.

What tends to happen to women, or even men who don't have these priorities in place is that, you may place that person on such a high pedestal that he can't even live up to those expectations. After a while, he will disappoint you. He is only human. You've had respect for him based on unrealistic capabilities, perhaps because you saw more in him than you saw in yourself. Once that disappointment happens repeatedly, then your relationship may suffer from what seems to be irreparable damage. He's not completely to blame. Your image of him was unhealthy. Reverence for your man is a good thing but he is no super hero and he is certainly no god. Now on the other hand, you need not waste your time with men you don't respect. You cannot polish him and grow him up. That is not your job. If you take that on as a job you will eventually wish you had not applied.

An Object Of Inspiration

We've heard the phrase "object of desire". The object of inspiration is someone who, without necessarily, trying, just inspires you to become a better you. We should all be so lucky to have someone like that. Not as a crutch or not even a mentor, necessarily, but just someone who gives you drive. I believe for both women and men it's nice to have someone who inspires us to push ourselves to higher levels. Even if you are intrinsically motivated we can all feel a little sluggish and uninspired at times. The operative word is, "inspire". It is sort of a gentle encouragement or perhaps even a little tough love at times but even then, the timing is just right. It is usually someone with whom you are impressed. Your children or parents may have that effect on you but as it pertains to a love interest, the emotion behind the motive is quite different.

I think many of us do not have this kind of relationship with our mates because of our own self-image. Well if you think about it for a minute, those people who make a good impression on us also inspire us to grow or to change. If nothing else they give us hope. Perhaps their accomplishments, wisdom and intelligence attract us. We see in them, greatness. Perhaps we see in them all we aspire to be. Maybe we have put that person on so high a pedestal that we may see ourselves as unworthy or inadequate by comparison. Maybe as a woman you've gone through life surrounded by many strong women. In my own life, there were no positive male figures around. If there was one he didn't play any significant role in my life.

So, if you're like me, and there are some, you're the kind of woman that has low expectations of men. You had little or no experience with the kind of man you really think is ideal so why dream about this superficial superman character.

Whatever life experience influenced your limited and pessimistic view of men, it serves as a hindrance. This is true for many people, including men who have no respect for women. In which case, you will not attract anyone that impresses you. You accept low standards because you expect them. Maybe you even subconsciously prefer them to be less than wonderful, because then they won't call you to higher standards. It's kind of like the thought of being a billionaire. Of course it would be nice and could even be attained, but many people would not dare to even dream that big. I said all this to say, you could be blocking your own blessing when it comes to matters of the heart. It has been said, we attract that which we feel we deserve. I believe subconsciously we do. Unfortunately, what we really feel we deserve is not really what we want. We tend to think what we really want is an unrealistic possibility for us. How many times have you been in a relationship and said to yourself, I deserve better? Well simply stop settling for less. On the other hand, perhaps you're in a relationship and you feel like they have lowered their standards to be with you. If that is the case, watch how you respond to them. Your insecurities will run them away. It goes back to you feeling whole and worthy of good things and believing you are capable of greatness. It all starts with you!

Do Value Your Mate's Opinion?

Here is a sure test of whether or not you are with someone for whom you have reverence. If you frequently find yourself completely disregarding your significant others opinion, just how significant is he? Maybe it's not you. Maybe he has too little input to regard. Either way, I'm going to go out on a limb and assume you are in a very unfulfilling relationship.

We come from many different backgrounds and those experiences from as far back as our conscience can remember, shape and mold our perceptions, our expectations, our aspirations and ultimately our actions. I find that out of many of the women I've met, the kind of woman that is more likely to seek the opinion of her man, (that is if she really likes him) is the woman who is or was a daddy's girl. She's grown up watching her father take care of his family even to the point of sacrificing his own needs. Maybe even her grandfather had a significant influence on her. She's empathetic of the male struggle and even deeply grounded in her belief to stand by him. Moreover, mom has always held dad in high regard. She perhaps follows in her mother or grandmother's footsteps. She has old fashion values and believes the man is head of the household. I am not referring to, nor encouraging anyone to tolerate being bullied or intimidated in any way. If you are in a relationship with someone who dominates you and dictates to you and you listen because you're afraid of him that is a different story. I can only say, leave that relationship...Yesterday! Then there is another kind of woman. I can personally relate with this woman. She has had to hold it together for everyone in her household, in all aspects, she's watched her mother do it. As I have mentioned before this is the woman for whom there were no positive male role models. She's not necessarily against standing by her man or even being the woman behind him, but her training was different. It was harder. She is not much of a follower. She has been the leader. If a man wants her to follow, he has to bring his "A" Game! He has to show up in every situation as a willing soldier on the front line, suited for battle.

Many people don't know why they are the way they are. Many people don't recognize their own influence on the negative outcomes they experience. That is the biggest reason they are stumbling over the same road blocks repeatedly. In order to remember what you need, it helps to know why you need it in the first place. The idea behind valuing your mate's opinion is really to benefit you. If you repeatedly find yourself in a relationship with someone you don't feel is the right one for you, you have to know that speaks volumes about you as a person. What is it saying?…Well, that is what you need to figure out. You should be with someone you are proud to be with. Don't just settle for someone who makes you feel good about yourself because they don't call you to a higher standard. To value your mate's perspective on things is to feel connected to their way of thinking. It is also a way to insure that you don't get too complacent in life because they are more likely to push you to be your best. Ideally, you will feel like that about one another. If not the balance of the relationship is off and so will be the partnership. Ask yourself is this person someone I don't want to live without or do they just fit the checklist? If you're with someone whose perspective is never valuable to you, that's probably not "the one". Not everyone who solicits your attention should win the opportunity to be your mate. I know relationships take work but love and respect are not the things you should be working on. Those are innate and organic qualities that someone else has to inspire you to feel. It is the love and respect you have for a person that compels you to work on your differences. You may even have to work on your passion after a period of time or your friendship but I contend that love and reverence is the motive behind the will to do it. Those two, should already be in tact.

The Importance Of The United Front

The united front is all about showing respect for the relationship itself. In case you're not familiar with the term united front, it means to present a strong sense of unity. In the eyes of observers, a couple should appear to be an unbreakable bond. Observers respect and admire an unbreakable bond. People are reluctant to try to break a strong bond. Therefore, couples should most certainly not display their insecurities or disregards for one another in front of others. Arguments, major disagreements, feuding, disrespect, or anything that may help outsiders identify disconnections in the bond. Although it is natural for couples to have disconnection and disagreements, it only exacerbates your problems when you invite others to view them. Your problems and disagreements are almost as private as your sex-life. That is privileged information. Don't put your business out there! Whom ever you choose to vent to, should be a carefully selected few.

This is true for more reasons than one. If it is your loved ones, perhaps your sister, brother, or parents with whom you share your relationship woes, you will create a negative image of your mate to them. They have your best interest at heart. They will naturally begin to develop dislike for anyone who appears to negatively affect your well-being. Later, when you have kissed and made-up and you want to share your joys they can't get over the woes. They don't know which to believe. They cannot help but question, are you in a good relationship or a bad one? In our anger, we can be pretty good about tearing someone down. In our version of the story, we are the victim, the hero, the one who did everything right...well, to an audience of family or close friends you are very convincing! Their bias is in favor of you. You're going to have a tough time convincing them the bad guy is now a good guy once you have made up and have a different perspective.

If your audience is the children to whom you are both the parents, your confrontations make them very uncomfortable to say the least. In some cases, it makes them petrified. They want to see the two people they look up to and depend on the most, laughing and loving, and working in unison. When children see their parents, loving and supporting one another, it gives them a stronger sense of security. For one, they do not have to take sides nor do they want to take sides. Another reason parents have to present a united front for the children is so the children know they can't play one parent against the other. They have to think their parents operate as co-pilots and they support each others decisions. I did say think! You don't have to agree on everything but you need to hold your peace until you can discuss it in private. By the way, private conversations are not private if they become so loud other people can hear them.

Another important reason for the keeping a united front is to minimize negative influence from outside sources. There are always going to be those who like to expose your weaknesses. Unhappy people don't want to feel unhappy alone. Just for the sake of familiarity, they would like to highlight how much your relationship is no better than theirs, or not as perfect as everyone thought. Even if it's true, if it's not bad enough for you to get out of it keep your issues private. A person, who is coveting another person's spouse or mate, loves to see imperfections in the relationship. They prey on, and feed off it. No matter how upset you get, act like you are in support of your mate in the presence of viewers. Grin and bear it until you have privacy...complete privacy.

Relationships can have enough obstacles to overcome without the added affects of negativity from outsiders. Having others add fuel to the fire is an obstacle you can do without. Other people's influence on your opinions and emotions toward your mate may create tribulation your relationship cannot overcome. If you need someone to voice your frustrations to it should be someone with little or no bias either way. It should be someone who can be a voice of reason who can look at the situation objectively without personal opinions. It should be someone who can be a good listener. Choose a neutral person who does not try to fix it. That person should be someone mature enough to understand that you're just venting. Most importantly, your "go-to" person should be someone who will keep your business as private as you need to keep it. I know this is easier said than done. Often times it is like reflex to become extremely angry in response to something your mate just said or done. You may feel the need to talk to someone to calm yourself, just be careful of whom you choose.

Another good reason to keep your composure is to avoid embarrassing each other. You do not want to be in connection with humiliating memories for the one you love. Your name should not be synonymous with humiliation or embarrassment.

That can create a break down in the friendship, trust, respect and most certainly your intimacy. Even if they really deserve to be embarrassed and humiliated, if you're not ending the relationship, there's no benefit to taking that route.

THE JOY OF FULFILLING LOVE

THE JOY OF FULFILLING LOVE

We often think about protocol in relationships. That is, what we should do or what someone else should do if they are a wife or a husband or what is acceptable in a relationship. Ladies! We have our ideas about what a man ought to do on a date. Men have their own pre-conceived notion of the "marrying type". Certainly there are rules to this thing but if you're sitting down thinking about rules in your relationship, then you're grasping at the wrong straws because something may be missing but it has nothing to do with rules. No relationship is perfect, but there are two things a couple should aspire for, these things are Resonance and Synergy. I know you're saying—What? I've given this a lot of thought and I've come to believe these are the necessary traits that provide the currents that give relationships longevity and without them sooner or later the love affair will flat-line. Resonance and Synergy are just scientific terms to describe things that produce greater results simply because they are connected. Writing the rules and combining your resources according to what helps you grow as a couple is the general idea.

Resonance; *is the state of a system in which an abnormally large vibration is produced in response to external stimulus occurring, when it is subjected to vibration from another source at or near its own natural frequency.* In other words, two objects that have similar tendencies will greatly increase those tendencies when they operate near or with one another. Resonance is the result of having, chemistry, commitment, compromise and friendship. It is ease brought on by working in partnership. For example when a child is on a swing and she is pushing her feet forward as the swing goes forward and back as the swing goes back then the frequency of her movements are in resonance with the frequency of the swing. The result is, the swing goes higher and faster without any strain on the swing or the child. When two things are in motion and in harmony with one another, they become like one moving force. They are a strong force together, each following the flow of its natural movements. Therefore, no strain is on one more than the other. However, the two get increased energy from the other. Neither can operate at this amplified frequency without the other.

Synergism; *is the interaction of elements that when combined produce a total effect that is greater than the sum of the individual elements contribution.* When these elements are combined, they increase one another's effectiveness. For instance, the strength of one magnet probably couldn't pick up a large metal plate but several magnets can do it with ease. Synergism, is the product of putting your assets and efforts together as explained in nurturing and compromise. In essence, when you combine the strength of many strong attributes they yield a much greater outcome than one can alone. When a couple works in partnership by bringing their best to the unit, they can become a power couple. If one is good with finances then both their finances should reflect that. Therefore, the individual who is bad at money management should be willing to relinquish that control to the one who handles it better.

There shouldn't be one with good credit and the other with bad credit or one who has to suffer a life of debt because of an irresponsible mate. This can happen when we look at our relationship as though it should be a team effort. On a team, each member has his task to perform which is fine for a team. The problem is, in a team if one member is not doing his or her job well, it will affect the whole team and eventually he gets voted out and replaced. When it comes to teams, that is an okay strategy for a team. If you go into your relationship thinking like a team player your relationship may suffer the same fate as many teams...eventually having to get a new member.

The relationship is a partnership. Where partnerships are concerned, there is a joint effort because there is a joint risk. Each partner is aware that each has different strengths. However, it is in the best interest of the union, that they are knowledgeable and willing to step into whatever role the situation calls for. Partners, unlike team members have a joint investment. investment. They will suffer the same fate if the business should fail. Therefore, bring your all to the unit for the sake of the whole unit because as it prospers you will too.

Relationships of the past, unlike relationships today, stayed together because couples depended on one another. Today, we are all doing our own thing. We get married but our purpose in life, our goals and ambitions never marry. The thing we focus on the least at the beginning of a relationship, is that lasting partnerships need purpose. In many cases that never comes into focus at all. When our relationships have purpose beyond our emotional needs it is less vulnerable. Feelings are not enough to sustain the bond it needs other systems of support. If we only invest into our emotional fulfillment we weaken the commitment because emotions are volatile. Therefore we have to focus on a purpose beyond personal fulfillment or even personal accomplishments. I'm not saying there's anything wrong with being able to hold things together on your own, but if your motive is to protect yourself in the event of separation, you'll make it a self-fulfilling prophecy. The very act of building the cushion will simultaneously create the fall.

Couples need to have a certain level of need for one another to strengthen the bond so it's not easy to walk away. When it's easy to walk away, we separate and divorce without thinking things through. Then once things are calm, you may find it wasn't so bad. Relationships cannot rely solely on emotional connection to keep them alive. The investment has to be bigger than that.

It is good to be physically attracted to someone and it is good when they can make you laugh. However, at the end of the day when life feels like too much for one person to handle alone, you need a partner. A companion is nice but a partner gets down in the trenches with you. When things are not so pretty, because life can and will bring hard times, you deserve a partner. Know what you have, do not convince yourself that it's something it's not, simply because you are desperate for more. It begins with you. Do not compromise your essence. Know your path in life and be sure when you meet that potentially special someone they know their own path in life. Just as a person has a divine purpose as an individual so should a couple. Couples should have common goals something they aspire for as a unit. Not only for personal gain or simply building a life together but also for a much greater affect on the world at large. After all, our gifts and talents are not given to us just so we can live better ourselves, but we were meant to touch the lives of others.

There it is! It has come down to these two things, Resonance and Synergy; these are the byproducts of having fulfilled the Hierarchy. Once all your ducks are in a row, the path is clear, the transition is smoother and your efforts produce phenomenal results. The result is not a flawless, not even an obstacle-free relationship but one of unity, respect, friendship and most of all lasting love.

Making It Personal

When we experience symptoms that make us feel less than our best, to find a cure it helps us to be able to identify the symptoms with a name. I have said, I'm not the first to try to figure this "love thing" out. There is one theory that I found interesting that gives the short version of the many relationship types. This theory gives a name to the issues in our relationships, that prevent us from connecting on the deepest level.

It is the *Triangular Theory of Love,* by Psychologist Robert Sternberg. According to Sternberg's theory, love is comprised of three components. The amount of love a person experiences depends on the strength of these three components and the kind of love depends on their strength relative to each other. The three components are intimacy, passion and commitment.

1. *Intimacy* encompasses feelings of connectedness, closeness and bondedness.

2. *Passion* encompasses the drives that lead to romance, physical attraction and sexual consummation.

3. *Commitment* encompasses, in the short-term, the decision that one loves another, and in the long-term the commitment to maintain that love.

I wanted to bring this theory to your attention because Hierarchy of Love proposes to show you how to accomplish the fullness of a loving relationship. The Triangular Theory of Love, I think, can better help you identify under what category your relationship falls. In hopes to help you gain some advantage over your obstacles, I thought another perspective could be valuable. If you would like to read the full journal of this theory, you can find a journal/article on Sternberg's Triangular Theory of Love on the American Psychological Associations website. www.apa.org.

According to the Triangular Theory:

- nonlove; is one that lacks intimacy, passion and commitment.
- Liking/Friendship; exist in true friendships. It is one that is high in intimacy but lacking passion and commitment.
- *Infatuated love*; is pure passion usually present in the beginning of romantic relationships. It has passion but lacks intimacy and commitment.
- *Empty love*; such as that in the Hierarchy's contractual agreement, has commitment and lacks passion and intimacy.
- *Romantic love*; has intimacy and passion but no commitment. This is a bond fueled by emotions of passion and arousal.

- *Companionate love*; has intimacy and commitment but lacks passion. This is another example of contractual agreement.
- *Fatuous love;* is one in which commitment is motivated by the passion but there is a lack of intimacy.
- *Consummate love*; is the complete form of love, the ideal love. A consummate love according to Sternberg is one where the couple, over the long-term can't imagine their lives with anyone else.

Whichever category your relationship falls under right now is likely to change overtime. Relationships can go from one category to the next many times throughout the course of the courtship or marriage. It is important to note that a relationship cannot be built on emotion alone. As crazy as that sounds, I have to reiterate, building a relationship on the basis of emotional needs alone creates and unstable union. Our emotions are wishy washy and they encourage bias opinions and selfish acts. Neither can it be all about duties and responsibilities because we simply cannot completely ignore our feelings and desires. I want to give you the tools to help you find where you are in your relationship so you can use what you know to enrich your relationship, either the current one or a future one.

The rank of the hierarchy falls as such; fulfilling love is the goal. It is the piece that adorns the structure when everything else is complete and well built. But before you can reach it, there has to be partnership of mutual respect. There has to be a since of security that your partner has your back, in any situation, in order for you to consider that person a partner. Therefore you have to be consistent, empathetic, and selfless to build trust.

We have to also like each other. We must enjoy each other's company so we have to build a friendship. And we must not discount the need for sex appeal for it is the thing that sustains desire. We have to keep it alive to keep the relationship's heart beating…so to speak. But before we can think of any of these things we must be in tune with ourselves, mature, stable and self secured. The components to build the relationships must be built in concert with one another. I am most certain that if either of these components is missing in a relationship, the relationship will be affected sooner or later. If one individual feels a void in any area the relationship subsequently suffers from that void as well. Ignoring the void soon becomes like a chronic illness, sooner or later it demands attention and we can either address it or let it suck the life from the relationship.

Having a strong bond in one area does not serve as a complete filler to keep other areas from breaking down. It doesn't matter how sweet you are or how good you think you've been to a person or how good looking you are, the key is this, in a nutshell; those things you want your partner to feel for you, you have to inspire it. Just like a lock, you can't open it without the right combination applied in the necessary order.

No need to try to figure out who's right or wrong. All you need to know is no one can impact your partners feelings about you like you can. It may sound cruel but if they're not feeling you it's really not their fault. Honestly, if you think about it, just like we cannot turn the love off at will, we cannot turn it on at will either. Therefore, the ball is in your court. If you want the total package, if you want the best of your partner's love, the hierarchy must be in place.